THE SEVEN SEAS

"When You and I behind the Veil are past,
Oh, but the long, long while the World shall last,
Which of our Coming and Departure heeds,
As the Seven Seas should heed, a pebble-cast."

EDWARD FITZGERALD
from The Rubaiyat of Omar Khayyam (1st ed.)

In Memoriam
JOHN LELLO (1929-2017)

THE SEVEN SEAS
Voyages in Verse and Colour

Poems by JOHN ELINGER
Illustrations by SANDRA LELLO

SIGNAL BOOKS
Oxford

First published in 2021 by
Signal Books Limited
36 Minster Road
Oxford
OX4 1LY
www.signalbooks.co.uk

A catalogue record for this book is available
from the British Library.

ISBN 978-1-909930-81-0 Paper

Design and production: *Baseline Arts Ltd*
Illustrations: *Sandra Lello*
Printed in India

CONTENTS

FOREWORD BY *Wendy Ball* 7

INTRODUCTION 10
1. The Ocean Today 10
2. The History of the Ocean 18
3. The Sea Routes 26
4. The Choice of Sights 32
5. The Poems 34
6. The Paintings 38
7. Afterword 42

1. THE NORTH ATLANTIC OCEAN 45
2. The Mediterranean Sea and THE INDIAN OCEAN 71
3. THE ANTARCTIC OCEAN 97
4. THE SOUTH ATLANTIC OCEAN 115
5. THE SOUTH PACIFIC OCEAN 135
6. THE NORTH PACIFIC OCEAN 153
7. THE ARCTIC OCEAN, the Baltic and the North Sea 175

ENVOI 196

Acknowledgements 198

FOREWORD

SEVENTH HEAVEN

One planet earth; two eyes and ears to know
its rich variety; three habitats
for living things – the air, the land, the sea;
four seasons, four directions – north, south, east
and west, four gospels, four dimensions: length,
breadth, height – and time (like space, a mystery!);
five...stones, wits, fingers, senses (five-a-day?);
six swans a-swimming, six bright shiners, throw
a six to start, six of the best, sixth form,
six shooters...not a happy number! But
the number seven's special: seven days –
a week, the Seven Planets, Seven Stars,
the Seven Virtues – and the Seven Sins,
the Wonders of the World, and don't forget
the Seven Ages of mankind...but we
would rather celebrate in paint and verse
the seven continents, and Seven Seas.
The Seventh Heaven's here, or nowhere, found.

I was deeply honoured when the publisher, James Ferguson, asked me to write the Foreword for this delightful book. The author and the illustrator each wanted someone famous, like David Attenborough or Ellen MacArthur – or even Marco Polo or Christopher Columbus – but they were all otherwise engaged. I think the illustrations are superb, and the verse is (as a reviewer of one of the earlier volumes in the series carefully observed) 'adequate'. I know both the poet ('reader, I married him', over 60 years ago!) and the painter.

My husband and I met Sandra and John Lello on a cruise a few years ago, and we became good friends. *The Seven Seas* is dedicated to his memory, for John Lello sadly died while the book was still *in utero*. I think he would have loved it – and proof-read it severely! (As I, also, have done.)

The poet was raised on the books of Arthur Ransome ('better drowned than duffers – if not duffers, won't drown') and agrees wholeheartedly with Kenneth Grahame's opinion that 'There is nothing – absolutely nothing – half as much worth doing as messing about in boats'. He, and his siblings and cousins, built a Kon Tiki log raft as children, and successfully sailed it across a lake in Wales, and later constructed (from a kit – sail and all) a little dinghy they called Hob. He taught me to sail during our engagement; I said that if he capsized with me on board I would cancel the wedding! He was careful. He captained his college's sailing team at Oxford, and sailed a Firefly in the national championships at Weymouth in 1958 (best result, 94th: I was his crew that day!). A few years later, he and I sailed 30-footers on the Norfolk Broads, with our baby on the deck in her playpen, and (being purists – no engine) succeeded in the rare challenge of transferring from the northern to the southern rivers (and back again) at Great Yarmouth, using only our mud-anchor and the turning tide. (Read *The Big Six* for Ransome's account of that manoeuvre.) And we lived for a year like hippies on a converted Thames barge moored in Chelsea. (It sank!)

[8]

Later, seduced by the delights of ocean- and river-cruising, we took the opportunity to sail whenever and wherever we could – in Wales, the Caribbean and Sydney harbour, for example. In recent years, 'John' has trained to become a skipper of boats for hire on inland waterways, rivers and canals, and proudly shows off at every opportunity his Master's Certificate – which is, however limited to boats carrying no more than twelve passengers (on inland waterways)! Today, we have become 'frequent cruisers', sailing the world's oceans in big ships and luxury.

There is no finer way of enjoying the Third Age of life: it probably costs less than residence in an 'old people's home', and is much more fun (and the food's better!). But, temporarily we hope, the Covid crisis has kept us at home for the time being... We are spending the time in seeking to make our small contribution to meeting the 'Global Warming Crisis' with solar panels, a veganish diet, and so on. Greenpeace tells us to reduce our carbon footprint and 'tread lightly'. Conscious of the seriousness of the threat, especially to the oceans, the subject of this book, we have agreed to forgo air travel in future; we have never owned or driven a car; and we already have a 'two (born) child family' (with four more adopted children). This needs to become the new global norm (1-2 child families), if we seriously hope to restore the climate to a stable condition which will sustain life as we know it on land and in the sea.

This book, *The Seven Seas,* is a celebration of the sea, of exploration and seamanship, of marine flora and fauna, and of life on the ocean wave in ships large and small. It is a labour of love, dedicated (with our love) to John Lello. I know you will admire the illustrations, and hope that you will enjoy the thoughtful Introduction and the various topographical verses. Poems of place are out of fashion today – poetry is all about feelings – but they have a secure provenance in the great traditions of Classical and English verse. Look for the deeper tones of seriousness beneath the colourful surfaces of words and images: concerns about global warming, cultural conflicts, and the pollution of the oceans, alongside the age-old challenges of inequality and persecution. This is a book designed, like all good art, to delight (of course), to teach (as well, or so the poet hopes), and (possibly) to transform the lives of those who read it. Remember the Silver Rule: 'First, do no harm'. Or learn the difference between a sonnet and a sestina. Or just enjoy it!

WENDY BALL

[9]

INTRODUCTION

I. THE OCEAN TODAY

The world we dwell in's almost drowned by water:
earth's unique feature is the foaming ocean.
This land we live on's little more than quarter
as large as all those seas in endless motion.
The sea is salt – that will not lose its savour,
though daily filled afresh by rains and rivers.
The sea's a threat – where even brave men quaver
before the storm: winds rise, the rigging quivers,
the skies grow darker, sometimes big ships founder,
while waves like mountains mutilate the seashore.
Old Neptune roars with rage and pride – he's drowned a
sailor, whose body's litter on a lee-shore.
    Although man thinks he's wise, and knows he's clever,
    today the ocean's still as fierce as ever.

SALT WATER COVERS ABOUT 70 PER CENT OF THE SURFACE OF THE EARTH. Our planet, the 'blue planet' (as seen from outer space, though it looks more like a blue marble to me!) might more aptly be christened the 'watery planet' in honour of its most distinctive feature, one that makes the earth unique within the solar system, and which provides an essential feature in an environment which can support life as we know it.

If the solid rock which forms the surface of the molten interior of the earth were of a uniform nature, there would be no land at all. The entire planet would be under water – more than a mile deep. Fortunately for us, the rock is of two broadly different types, basaltic and granitic. The former is denser and heavier than the latter; consequently granitic areas float on the liquid interior of the earth at a higher level than the basaltic regions. The oceans fill the basaltic troughs; we live on the solid granitic land masses – although continental drift, leading to 'folding', and volcanic activity have raised areas of the sea-bed to the surface. Britain was once part of such a submerged region.

From the point of view of life, and living things like plants and animals, the earth provides a happy balance of several important controlling conditions: most notably, the sun's heat, the earth's gravitational strength, and its magnetic field. The first of these ensures that most of the H_2O on our planet remains in a liquid state – though the polar regions are covered in ice, and the skies are filled with clouds, reminding us that were we nearer to, or further from, the sun our precious water would be turned to vapour, or ice. And if gravity on earth was as weak as it is on the moon, the water vapour in the clouds would float away into space, gradually depriving the earth of its most distinctive feature, and rendering it inhospitable to life. The earth's powerful magnetic field prevents the solar winds from stripping away the ozone layer (as has happened on Mars, for example) which provides a shield against harmful ultra-violet rays. Scientists, who like to compete with the poets on occasions, refer to this happy cluster of factors which has facilitated life on earth as the 'Goldilocks Zone'. The faithful instance it as a further proof of the existence of God.

[11]

Sea water is salty. As we learn at school, that is because the rivers that feed the oceans carry sediment from eroded rock which includes soluble salts. However, the salinity of the ocean reached a steady-state many millions of years ago – unlike the Dead Sea and other land-locked inland lakes, the Great Salt Lake in Utah, for example, which are still growing saltier every year. The explanation for this apparent contradiction is that most of the rivers that feed the oceans today run over land that once formed the sea-bed, and has no more salt to yield, while the salt lakes receive their water from areas that have never been part of the ocean-floor. Salt water is denser than fresh water, making it easier for animals like us to float in, but that minor advantage is outweighed by the fact that it is undrinkable. 'Water, water everywhere – nor any drop to drink!'

The ocean covers almost 140 million square miles; its total volume is nearly 330 million cubic miles; its average depth is just over 12,000 feet. But, relative to the size of the planet, the ocean is more like a shallow puddle than a deep well. Nonetheless, the topography of the ocean-floor, could we but see it, would appear more dramatic and extreme than the land it surrounds. Mount Everest rises to 29,000 feet; the deepest ocean-trench reaches 36,000 feet below sea-level. The average height of the land area is 2,760 feet; the average depth of the ocean is almost five times greater – nearly two and a half miles.

It is traditional, and convenient, to think of the ocean as comprising seven mighty basins: the Arctic and the Antarctic Oceans surrounding the north and south poles; the Indian Ocean; the North and South Atlantic, and the North and South Pacific, Oceans – conventionally divided in either case by the equator. We have followed this scheme in the design of this book. These are the 'Seven Seas' of Fitzgerald's verse (1859) and Kipling's book of poetry (1896).

Sea levels rise and fall over time. At present, all the basins are filled and overflowing onto the continental shelves surrounding them. With the melting of the polar ice from the effects of global warming, levels will continue to rise and probably flood more of the low-lying regions, such as parts of Holland and East Anglia, Venice or the Maldive Islands, unless science, political action and human ingenuity can reverse the process or defend the threatened areas. London's Thames Barrier (which will need to be extended before 2050) may be the shape of things to come all over the world by the end of the century.

The sediments accumulated on the ocean-floor reveal information both about the history of the ocean, and of the effects of human activity today. Close to the sea-shore the strength of the currents determines whether the floor (and beach) are formed of stones and bare rock, or sand and mud. Strong currents stir up, suspend and carry fine material into deep water. The same effect is found in the deeper ocean, where substantial areas are free of sand and mud, in spite of the huge quantity of such material in the sea as a whole. We should be grateful for the weak currents that preserve the beaches for holiday-makers.

But we might be concerned (if we could see it) by the evidence of human activity revealed by trails of ash and coke along the principal sea-lanes used by steamers in the past, and by the litter deposited irresponsibly in rivers, and overboard at sea, creating dangerous levels particularly of plastic waste throughout the ocean. It is estimated that 5.25 trillion items of plastic waste were added to the contents of the oceans in 2016, and that eight million tons is deposited annually in the Mediterranean Sea alone. Our best hope seems to be the development and deployment of a plastic-eating microbe which could help to clean up the oceans that have been used (and abused) for centuries as sewage-farms and rubbish dumps.

The salinity (salt-content) of the ocean is fairly uniform at about 3.4%: water of this consistency freezes at 28.7° Fahrenheit, or just above -2° Centigrade. At its hottest (in the Persian Gulf in midsummer) the sea sometimes reaches a temperature of 90° Fahrenheit (about 32° C) at the surface. But, of course, the deeper areas are much cooler. As a result, the average temperature of the ocean is 39° F, or about 4° C. The main source of the sea's heat is the sun, which warms the upper layer (about five feet) of water in the ocean. The warmed surface, in turn, heats the atmosphere above it, producing warm westerly winds such as those which shape the climates of California, or the British Isles – but also creating (and reinforcing) violent storms, such as the annual hurricanes of the North Atlantic which regularly ravage North America.

[13]

The sea is naturally coloured pale blue, like the sky (and our 'blue planet'), partly due to a process described as the molecular scattering of light, whereby the shorter wavelengths (at the blue end of the spectrum) become scattered more than the longer wavelengths. But much of the perceived colour of the sea is created by the reflection of the sky above – blue on a fine day, grey under cloud-cover. See for yourself. Where plankton, sediments or decaying vegetation are abundant, the sea can show a greenish, or brownish, tinge – usually near the coastline. In certain conditions, the sea appears fluorescent, a phenomenon that occurs in both inorganic matter (like salt water) and the biosphere, when natural (ultraviolet) light invisible to humans is absorbed and then re-emitted at a lower wavelength within our visual range. (Of course, that's not the whole story: ask an expert.)

The oceans are subject to movement of several kinds, produced by tides, currents, river-estuaries, prevailing winds and the Coriolis Force, perhaps the most mysterious of all the external influences on the seas. Tidal variation is the most obvious evidence of the sea's incessant mobility. It is not rocket-science to realise that the tides are related to the rotation of the earth, the phases of the moon – and, less obviously, to the position of the sun in relation to the earth. Isaac Newton was the first scientist to develop a workable theory of tidal motion, though he overlooked the Coriolis Force.

On average, high tides occur every 12 hours and 25 minutes – which is half the time taken by the moon to *appear to* orbit the earth. Q.E.D. (The apparent rising and setting of the moon, of course – like that of the sun – is mainly caused by the earth's rotation: the moon takes a 'lunar month' – 28 days – to complete its actual orbit of the earth.) Tidal range – the rise and fall between high and low tides – also varies in accordance with the moon's phases. Around the British Isles, tides are most extreme just after the full, and new, moons; they show the least range when the moon appears to us as a semi-circle. Similarly, we observe higher tides at the sun's equinoxes; lower ones at the solstices. Tidal variation, as we observe it, is caused by the combined gravitational attraction of the sun and the moon, as they move within their orbits, in relation to the earth, as it rotates – acting on the mobile oceans. (The rest is mathematics.)

[14] The sea is affected by a large number and variety of currents, both horizontal and vertical. Some are more or less permanent, like the Gulf Stream or the Humboldt Current; others are temporary and disappear when the driving force, wind or tide, changes. For example, at the coast one can find a regular pattern of onshore winds by day and offshore winds at night, caused by the sea gaining and losing its heat more slowly than happens on land. River estuaries generate currents: the effect of the Amazon can be seen for several miles from the coastline. A study of the seven oceans confirms that the traditional division of the Atlantic and Pacific at the equator is a faithful representation of their separate systems of circulating currents. Currents also rise and fall vertically – for example, when the deep sea meets a land-mass where the prevailing off-shore wind blows warm surface water away from the coast: the result is 'up-welling' of cooler water from below.

The Coriolis Force (I'm glad you asked!) is created by the rotation of the earth: its effect is strongest at the poles, and weakest at the equator. The result is a southward drift in the southern hemisphere, and a northward flow in the northern hemisphere. Since the earth rotates towards the east, giving us the impression that the sun is moving westwards during the day, the Coriolis Force circulates water clockwise to the north, and counter-clockwise to the south, of the equator. But don't try this at home: basins and baths are not large enough to provide a satisfactory demonstration of this effect. Gustave-Gaspard Coriolis was the French engineer who first explained the force in 1835.

Apart from H_2O, sea-water contains a large number of minute quantities of many of the common elements, beside sodium (in the form of its chloride, common salt): potassium, magnesium, calcium and strontium (among many others). The soluble salts of these elements give the sea its distinctive taste. Also found in water are important elements that nourish plant-growth (for example, phosphorus, nitrogen and silicon) and dissolved gases, of which carbon dioxide is perhaps the most interesting and important, since it is such a key factor in plant nutrition and the greenhouse effect. The oceans even contain gold – in minute quantities. We might extract one ounce from eight million tons of sea-water, having first isolated about 280,000 tons of soluble salts!

The sea is a more hospitable environment for both plants and animals than is the land – in the sense that marine conditions show less variation than we find on land, and therefore require less adaptability from living organisms. The range of temperature (40° F) and the variation (at most, 15° F a year) is lower than it is on shore, where these figures can exceed 100° F; and the abundance and buoyancy of water enable the plants (like seaweed) to dispense with root-systems, and organisms like jelly-fish to live without skeletons. Whales may grow to be as much as 100 ft long and weigh up to 100 tons: on land such creatures would crush their own limbs. Evolution does not favour obesity (for long): remember the dinosaurs!

[15]

The sea is inhabited by a wide range of living organisms, microbes, marine plants and animals. Indeed, almost half of the world's animal-classes are found only in the oceans, and over 90 per cent of them occur somewhere in the sea. These include fish, reptiles, birds, and mammals – both semi-aquatic (like seals, for example) and fully aquatic (whales and porpoises). There are numerous examples of highly-specialised species, like the corals, star-fish and crustaceans – including barnacles, crabs, lobsters, mussels, and many other varieties. One of the most remarkable features of the processes of evolution (and adaptation) of life-forms is the extraordinary variety of species that find a niche for survival in the earth's multiplicity of environments.

Most of these marine animals reproduce by the emission of eggs, which may be fertilised internally or externally. In either case, there may (or may not) be provision of some early parental care and protection. Where both internal fertilisation and (some) parental care are the rule, the offspring number no more than a few hundred at each conception. Where neither is provided, the hopeful eggs number several million. In mammals, like us, the number of eggs produced by the female is limited, both by frequency of ovulation (roughly once a month) and duration (the menopause), reflecting the devoted parental care provided both before and after birth by mammalian females: in contrast, the males seem to be able to generate almost unlimited sperm throughout their lifespan. (And we still have much to learn about child-care...)

Incidentally, it may be noted *en passant* that the 'Darlington hypothesis' (named after a sometime Professor of Geography at Oxford University) proposes that humans passed through an important evolutionary development period as semi-aquatic primates living in the estuaries of rivers in central Africa, where we acquired our upright posture and hairless bodies – and no doubt invented a primitive spear to catch fish for lunch. If 'race-memory' is real, then such an idea might help to explain our abiding love of the sea, its beaches – and water-sports of all kinds.

The ocean reveals a cycle of life reminiscent of the old song, 'On Ilkley Moor Baht 'At', whereby the plant-life feeds herbivorous creatures, like clams and oysters, which in turn become prey for the primary carnivores, like arrow-worms or baleen whales, themselves forming food for a chain of increasingly fearsome creatures – the higher carnivores, topped by the great white shark, and ourselves – which ultimately also die and decompose, to provide nutrients for the cycle to continue. 'Then we shall all 'ave etten thee!'

What about us? The oceans provide both an enormous resource and a mighty challenge for humanity. The sea is a vast storehouse of water and heat – and yet many brave or foolhardy mariners die there from thirst or cold. It has benefited island communities, enabling them, for example, to develop parliamentary democracy (like Iceland in 930, or Britain in 1275), while feudalism still prevailed on the continent. Similarly, the breadth of the Atlantic helped the United States of America to win their independence in 1776, while the narrow straits of the English Channel enabled Britain to withstand the assault of Nazi Germany in 1940.

But the sea is both a barrier and a means of transport and communication: the acquisition of a far-flung empire by the British depended on a powerful and effective navy in the long-past days when 'Britain rule(d) the waves'. The oceans feed us – and recycle our waste-products. The sea sustains a wide range of businesses, from fishing and mining to transport and cruising, and offers a challenging environment for our recreations and pastimes – sailing boats or building sand-castles, for example. The ocean is the source of fertilisers (like sea-weed and guano), salt, gas and oil (from the sea-floor), fish and pearls, among many other primary products.

Today, the ocean is both threatening and threatened, as never before. Global warming, which both heats the ocean (warmer water expands) and melts the ice-caps at the poles, is already beginning to raise sea-levels to heights which will flood substantial areas of land, destroying flora and fauna and driving human communities to find higher ground for resettlement. Experts tell us that the 'water-crisis' is the most serious global risk facing humanity today. In the 20th century the global population tripled: our use of fresh-water increased six-fold. Not only will it need to be rationed in the future, and shared more equitably, but we must also find new ways of extracting it from the sea – cheaply, and soon. Meanwhile, human activity and carelessness pollute the seas with plastic waste, rubbish and sewage.

Problems like these are man-made; they must be managed by human skill and resolve – or endured. The oceans will survive, whatever we do. The inconvenience (and the challenge) is ours – which seems fair enough, since we bear the responsibility for creating these problems – and for solving them, if we can, and choose to. But the oceans were here before we emerged from the complex processes of evolution – and they will still be there after we have gone the way of the dinosaur and dodo.

[17]

2. THE HISTORY OF THE OCEAN

But where, you ask, does all that water come from?
Our seas make earth unique amongst the planets –
alive with fish and seaweed, seals (and scum from
human pollution) whales, whelks, gulls and gannets.
Substance transforms: the water's made from gases.
Matter, not mind, endures: stuff is immortal,
although unstable. Water, ice, those masses
of cloud, presaging rain, a moment's thought'll
convince you are one thing – in transformation.
$e=mc^2$ reminds us: matter
and energy are in a like relation,
subject to permanent entropic scatter.
    Forget the facts of life – philosophy, biology:
      what's real are space and time – and physics, and cosmology.

EVERY SCHOOL-CHILD (WHO WATCHES TV) KNOWS THAT THE UNIVERSE BEGAN WITH A 'BIG BANG' almost 14 billion years ago, 14 million millennia, one hundred and forty million centuries, or 14 and nine noughts. A very long time indeed! (Experts now tell us that the 'big bang' was neither big, nor a bang. I wonder how they know?) We have today almost 5,000 years of recorded history: the universe is almost three million times older than the period our record of human progress covers. We are late-comers to space and time, which were here long before we arrived – and will still be here long after we have gone.

During the long gestation of the observable universe, a number of major events have occurred, which ultimately made our existence possible – including the formation of the galaxies, the establishment of the solar system, the cooling of the earth, the accumulation of water, the development of a breathable atmosphere, the origin of life, and the evolution of species of plants and animals – one of which is humanity, with our peculiar characteristics of intelligence, consciousness, imagination, choice, language, music, poetry and art...

The universe seems to be governed by a number of physical laws – including two which are particularly important for our understanding of what happens: the law of the indestructibility of matter, and the law(s) of gravity. Each of these plays a significant part in the story of the earth's oceans. Unlikely as it may seem, the force of gravity is thought to have concentrated all the matter in the universe into one tiny speck (of extraordinary density) – which then exploded (in the 'not so big bang') to create the expanding universe we can observe, and (partly) understand.

[19]

(One possible idea is that our expanding universe was preceded by a contracting one. And, just possibly, this sequence of contraction and expansion has recurred, and will recur, throughout eternity, if – as seems plausible – space and time are infinite and boundless. These concepts are difficult for us to contemplate, conditioned as we are by our short lives and small world. However, this cyclic model of the universe is only one of the competing theories under debate today. Nobody ever said science was simple!)

Be that as it may, about one billion years after the primal explosion the galaxies of stars began to form: our galaxy, the Milky Way, came into being about 10 to 11 billion years ago. But the Solar System (the sun, with its cluster of circulating planets) only started to take its existing shape some four and a half billion years ago: the sun seems to have evolved rather later than most stars. It is a 'secondary star', created by the explosion of a spent (primary) supernova. The oldest rocks on earth were formed soon afterwards – and primitive life emerged on earth remarkably soon after that, perhaps almost four billion years ago. Plant life evolved the process of photosynthesis by about 3.4 billion years before the present time (BP), and the atmosphere of the earth gradually became 'oxygenated' and breathable (by aerobic organisms like us) by 2.5 billion BP. (Photosynthesis is a process whereby the sun's energy is converted into a chemical form which can promote the life and growth of plants [and some bacteria and algae] by transforming water and carbon dioxide from the atmosphere into carbohydrate sugars, while releasing oxygen into the atmosphere we breathe: it is (directly or indirectly) essential to many (but not all) living organisms today.)

Insects, fish and land-plants appeared about half a billion years ago – so, by that time there must have been some water for the fish to swim in. Then came the reptiles, dinosaurs, birds and mammals in about 0.2 billion BP (some two hundred million years ago). Primates evolved later still, about sixty-five million years ago, from whom the apes emerged in about 15 million BP. But modern man, *Homo sapiens*, is a latecomer, joining the party a mere 200,000 years ago. Distinguished by our upright posture, opposable thumbs, (almost) hairless bodies, large brains and tool-making skills, humans like us set to work to invent clothing, cooking, agriculture and animal husbandry, weapons, tools and construction, language and the wheel – and the arts of music, painting and poetry. Modern (recorded) history begins about five thousand years ago – soon after the building of Stonehenge.

From that abbreviated account of the history and development of the world, as we know it, three salient and enigmatic questions emerge: how did life begin? When, and from whence, came the water? And, how is it that humans evolved our particular characteristics of intelligent consciousness, imagination and (at least) the illusion of choice. We are the only species we have ever come across that can ask, and seek to answer, questions like these. Each of these questions allows for two broadly different kinds of answer: *either*, life (and/or water, and/or *Homo sapiens*) came to the earth from elsewhere (Mars? another galaxy? other worlds in outer space, like Superman or ET?) as three possible examples of extra-terrestrial visitations... *or* these extraordinary features found on the earth evolved quite naturally here.

For the purposes of this book about the oceans, the questions of the origin of life, and of *Homo sapiens*, are not central – interesting though they undoubtedly are. We will adopt the assumption that life, as we know it, and mankind, as we understand ourselves, evolved on earth through the complex processes studied by biochemists and evolutionary scientists – not least, because the ET answer merely shifts the question to another planet in another galaxy: it doesn't answer it.

Some readers will think that religions can offer answers to these questions, but the statement, 'In the beginning God created the heavens and the earth...' (*Genesis*, I, i) invites the self-same objection as those from the realm of science-fiction: so, how did God come to exist? Nonetheless, religious accounts are not without their merits, if only to stimulate the poet and the artist (and composers, like Haydn, whose *Creation* is sublime). Indeed, the story of creation in chapter I of the Book of Genesis is a surprisingly apt account, given how ancient it is, of the development of the universe, the solar system, and life on earth, and – apart from placing the origin of plants (day 3) before the creation of the sun (day 4), which seems implausible – offers a striking (if poetic and fanciful) set of answers to the three big questions about the origin of life, of water, and of us.

But where did the water come from, and when did it form the seas, as we know them? Was it home-made, or imported? Neither of these possible answers turns out to be wholly wrong. Water-vapour is one of many substances floating around the universe and subject to gravitational capture by the stars and their planets. Earth's gravity is powerful enough, both to attract space-debris (like meteors, litter from space-stations, and gases) and to retain it. Indeed, it was possibly the capture of a meteor about 66 million years ago that did for the dinosaurs – and nearly wiped out the primitive primates too. *Caveat homo*. This process of gravitational capture has undoubtedly helped to create the earth's atmosphere, and contributed to the copious supply of water it holds. Some of the many comets drawn into the earth's orbit by its powerful gravitational force probably brought with them some water in liquid or (more likely) solid form.

[21]

But the origin of the sea, as we know it, and indeed of the all-important atmosphere we breathe, is unlikely to be wholly, or even mainly, due to extra-terrestrial importation. Under the influence of the unimaginably fierce temperatures and pressures generated by the 'big bang', and still at work in the sun (providing us with light and heat) and at the earth's molten core (as demonstrated by volcanic eruptions and earthquakes from time to time) – matter can be transformed in the ways the alchemists hoped to discover, to make gold from dross, diamonds from carbon, or even water from hydrogen and oxygen.

As the solar system took shape about four billion years ago, and the traditional nine planets (today we are told there are only eight, plus five 'dwarves'!) found their places around the sun, it seems that the earth underwent some dramatic changes over a relatively short period, creating the conditions that make life possible: cooling, rock-formation, the establishment of a stable atmosphere – and plentiful water – followed by the development of the earliest forms of living organisms, and plant-life utilising photo-synthesis, in about three billion BP.

'Bliss was it in that dawn to be alive,' as Wordsworth wrote.

It is interesting, and significant, that (so far) we have not detected life-forms on the other planets – remember the mnemonic: 'Surprisingly, Most Vegans Eat Mush Joyfully Sometimes – Unlike Normal People.' The solar system consists of the sun at the centre, Mercury, Venus, the Earth, Mars, Jupiter, Saturn, Uranus, Neptune, and Pluto – at the extreme edge (and no longer dignified as a true planet). Only the first four planets are close enough to the sun to be sufficiently warm to support life as we know it, but the range of temperature on Mercury and Venus seems too great, and the atmosphere on Mars too inhospitable (at least, today), for plants or living creatures to survive. Although water has recently been found in subterranean lakes on Mars, it still seems clear that our planet is a remarkable, perhaps unique, example of a 'Goldilocks Zone', hospitable to living things. Earth, the 'watery planet' with its breathable atmosphere, won the jackpot in the lottery of life.

[22]

We should try to imagine the conditions on earth during those early (half a billion, or so) years of its formation. The liquid, volcanic interior was constantly emitting streams and fountains of lava, ash, carbon dioxide, and water, to fill the primitive ocean basins and create the earliest (unbreathable) atmosphere. Clouds began to form, protecting the earth from some of the sun's fierce radiation. The temperature became stabilised, allowing primitive life-forms (and, later, plant-life) to emerge, which began to transform the atmosphere by reducing water to its constituent parts, and releasing oxygen to make possible the development of creatures that breathe – like us.

Since the ocean came into being and the basins were filled with water, the shape of the land-masses – and consequently of the ocean-basins themselves – has changed constantly, though very slowly, by a process called 'continental drift'. The earth's crust is made of a number of plates of different sizes, which fit together like a giant spherical jigsaw puzzle. There are eight major plates – and several more minor ones. These plates, which float on the earth's molten core, move slightly all the time, colliding with, rubbing against, and over-riding one another, so that the shapes of the continents change dramatically, if very gradually, from era to era.

Not until the geological age known as the Tertiary Period (as recently as five to two million years ago) would it have been possible to recognise the rough shape of the continents we find on our world-maps today. Before that time geologists assure us that the map would seem unrecognisable - with unknown continents like Gondwanaland, Laurentia and Pangea, for example, which no longer exist (as continents). For our purposes, the important point is that, although the ocean has been in existence for nearly four billion years, the seven basins ('the seven seas') began to take shape a good deal more recently than one hundred million years ago. The oceans adopted something like their modern configuration at much the same time that the earliest primates evolved.

One particularly dramatic and recent example of continental drift is provided by the sub-continent of India, a remnant of the lost continent of Gondwanaland, which had been slowly moving northwards through the Indian Ocean – until it collided with Asia about ten to twenty million years ago. This collision created the Himalayan mountain range, and the world's highest mountain, Mt. Everest. The sea itself, wind and rain are the primary agents of change in the landscape – and consequently of the shape of the oceans surrounding the continents. Rivers, glaciers, and the sea, constantly reshape the land through erosion, melt-water and flooding. Strong winds raise storms which submerge islands and destroy human settlements. Extremes of heat and cold create arid deserts and the ice-caps at the poles.

The character of the oceans has also been substantially, if subtly, transformed by the emergence of life and the diverse range of marine plants and animals which have made their homes within them. The Sargasso Sea, coral reefs and shoals of fish are but three striking examples of the visible evidence of marine life. The sea is alive with microscopic organisms, the colourful plants and creatures admired by scuba divers, and the dolphins, porpoises and whales that delight those who study the sea from the decks of cruise-ships.

[23]

The earliest humans, with their tool-making skills and drive to explore the unknown, soon learned to construct primitive rafts, canoes and dug-out boats to navigate the rivers and coastal waters. Our species succeeded in establishing settlements in every continent except Antarctica, and on most inhabitable islands, long before recorded history began some five thousand years ago. The cradle of mankind is located somewhere in central Africa: those early humans soon spread southwards and northwards to settle throughout Africa, Europe and Asia, but they needed boats to reach the Americas (though during the last ice-age, almost 12,000 years ago, a land-bridge existed between the eastern limits of Russia and western Alaska across the Bering Strait) and to settle in Australia, and on the myriad islands of the seven seas where people have dwelt for many generations. (We were all once refugees, asylum-seekers and immigrants.)

We know that the Viking long-ships reached America, Kon Tiki rafts crossed the Pacific, and the ancient Britons found a way across the Channel after the last ice-age had separated Britain from the continent.

(Before that time, Britain was joined to the continent, and presumably inhabited by early humans, who were driven, or frozen, out by the weather about 10,000 years ago.) For most of the last 200,000 years we have been mastering the skills of the oarsman and the sailor, the boat-builder and the navigator. Sea-power was essential (and still is) for defence and conquest, as the histories of ancient Greece, the Roman Empire, the rise of Venice, Spain and Britain, in turn, demonstrate. Most recently, control of the sea helped to determine the outcome of the two World Wars of the last century.

Human agency also bears a heavy responsibility for the state of the oceans today – both along the coastline and in deeper water. The Roman poet, Horace, wrote about two thousand years ago of the encroachment of the built environment into the domain of the sea: today, our species has virtually colonised the oceans with our oil-rigs, piers and docks, shipping of all kinds, both submarine and on the surface. Aircraft fill the skies and affront the silence of the seas. Pipelines, ash and rubbish disfigure the ocean floor. Our plastic waste thoughtlessly destroys marine life. As is so often the case, we have created the problem – and have the skill to solve it. But do we have the resolve to do so?

Our search for a coherent account of the history of the universe – its galaxies, and our solar system, of the earth's formation and development, and of the origin of the sea and its shaping into the seven ocean-basins we know today – has taken us from the realms of physics and cosmology to the science of chemistry and biology, geology and geography, and then (in the most recent period) to the evolution of mankind and the story of human activity and behaviour, as revealed in the disciplines of anthropology, history, economics, sociology, politics and psychology.

Looking forward as far into the future as we have been able to cast our eyes backward, we may imagine that this ideological journey will (like the expanding universe itself) switch into reverse – as our species becomes extinct (perhaps through the sun's increasingly fierce heat, if not by our own mistakes); and the earth (and sea) are swallowed up by a solar expansion, predicted to occur (don't hold your breath!) in about four and a half billion years from now; and the life of man – and life itself – will disappear (at least, on earth); so that the world, as we know it, becomes no more than an unrecorded footnote in an unwritten history of the universe – which will, nonetheless, continue to be driven by the laws of cosmology and physics, unobserved, purposeless, with neither beginning nor end. 'Our lives are empty, meaningless. We die', wrote the poet. The earth, our 'watery planet', the solar system, the Milky Way, the entire universe in its latest cycle, which we study and seek to understand, are also ephemeral, it seems.

3. THE SEA ROUTES

Sea-voyagers explore the restless ocean –
for what? some peace and rest from all this motion?
to find a fortune? or the Blessed Isles? –
and then set off again to face fresh trials.
He sails the seven seas for seven years,
forced to retreat whenever landfall nears,
confined to ocean, ice-floes, mist and winds.
Fleeing God's fury at his grievous sins,
the Flying Dutchman never comes to port
or touches land, except in dreams and thought.
We cruise around the world for several weeks,
watching the dolphins diving, the last streaks
of sunset, foam-tipped breakers, the new moon,
wild antics at the court of 'King Neptune'...
and hope these halcyon sea-days never end,
wishing our care-free cruise might yet extend
for ever. We feel envy for the man
from Holland – laze at leisure while we can:
the world of work and worry waits so near –
across that far horizon soon to appear.

OCEAN VOYAGES IN THE OPEN SEAS, OUT OF SIGHT OF LAND, HAVE BEEN ATTEMPTED — and completed — in every civilisation known to history for thousands of years. It would be wrong to imagine that sailors clung to the coast until our written records began in about 5,000 BP. The Phoenicians, for example, reached Cornwall (to buy tin) and the Vikings crossed the North Atlantic to establish settlements in Iceland, Greenland and North America. These early explorers seem to have navigated by the stars and 'dead reckoning' — a calculation of position by reference to direction and distance travelled (the latter deduced from measuring the boat's speed by means of a 'log' attached to a knotted rope). From this device the English language gained the words *log*, 'a record', and *knot*, 'measure of speed' (one nautical mile, i.e. one minute of latitude, about 1.12 land [or statute] miles, per hour).

The magnetic compass did not come into use until the 13th century CE. The first written reference to it was recorded by an Englishman, Alexander Neckam, who wrote in 1180 of 'a needle placed upon a dart, which sailors use to steer by when the (Great) Bear is hidden by clouds'. The 'compass' is, of course, the full range of the circular horizon, marked out on the card on which the magnetic needle was placed, but has come to refer to the entire instrument.

The constellation of Ursa Major, the Great Bear, provides two 'pointers' to direct the eye towards Polaris, the North Star — which is near, but not part of, what appears to modern eyes more like a Big Dipper than a Great Bear (in Chinese, the character that represents 'north' is partly formed from the character meaning 'ladle'). In the Southern hemisphere, where Polaris is hidden by the northern horizon, a similar calculation, using the Southern Cross, can establish the direction of true south.

Navigation has been transformed in modern times by advances in science and technology which have provided sailors with such devices as radar, sonar, radio communication, and the satnav. The development of air travel and the exploration of space have each contributed to transform navigation from the simple skills of the sailor to an exact science — and a marvel of modern technology. In a similar fashion, the early rough charts used by seamen have been replaced by maps of almost perfect accuracy in respect to distances, depths, routes, and dangers. Crossing the oceans is no longer the hazardous enterprise it once was.

And so, today, modern ships, whether carrying containers, oil, or tourists, travel to every part of the seven oceans where they can find safe harbourage, opportunities for trade, and sights for the visitors to wonder at.

However, nature is never completely tamed by human intelligence – as we learn afresh from time to time by the occurrence of hurricanes, tsunamis, earthquakes, storms, floods and landslides. The Titanic was sunk by a massive iceberg, and other great ships have come to grief on rocks and shoals in the modern era. *Cave marem.* All forms of travel, we must concede, carry with them a degree of risk – which, for the intrepid traveller, just adds a piquancy of excitement to the experience. Air-travel is convenient, when speed is of the essence; cruising is, arguably, the most delightful form of travel. (Neither is cheap: if you want to travel at low cost, you must get on your bike – or walk!)

The 'pleasure-cruising' industry began about 200 years ago with the formation of the Peninsular & Oriental Steam Navigation Company in 1822. P&O was primarily a mail-delivery service until the middle of the 19th century, when the company began to offer passenger cruise-trips from Southampton to exotic locations overseas, as well as fast passage between continents for those intent on business. In 1840 *Britannia*, the Cunard Line's first ship, left Liverpool with a cow on board to provide milk for the first-class passengers' afternoon tea on a 14-day transatlantic crossing. (The word *cruise* is borrowed from the Dutch, where it means 'cross'.)

These early cruise-liners were designed to provide both speed and luxury – although passengers in the 'steerage-class' were expected to bring their own food and bedding! Probably the most advanced design, and certainly the most ill-fated cruise-ship, was the *Titanic*, which sank after collision with an iceberg on its maiden voyage in 1912. (It is a sad irony that the *British Medical Journal* had earlier recommended sea-voyages for their curative and health-giving properties.) The period between the two World Wars of the 20th century witnessed the hey-day of luxurious pleasure-cruising, although the cruise-industry of today seems set to eclipse it. (During the wars a number of these great liners were requisitioned to act as troop-carriers: the soldiers found them quite comfortable.)

The development of fast, safe and regular services of travel by air in the middle of the 20th century proved a set-back for the passenger cruise-industry, which suffered a decline. Dictionaries and encyclopaedias of the period list *cruiser*, 'a warship designed for range and speed', but omit any mention of leisure-cruising. But the industry soon recovered, despite its focus moving from 'passenger-transport' to providing luxury 'floating hotels' for a growing number of pleasure-seekers from the leisured classes.

In this book, we take the reader on an imaginary, and wholly unperilous, journey around the seven oceans, starting and ending at Greenwich (the source of the Mean Line that provides the origin of our system of measurement of longitude and latitude) traversing the globe from north to south – and back again – and encircling the world three times, at (or near) the equator and around the southern and northern polar regions. We shall need neither compass nor a clear view of the stars at night – however, we have provided the reader with maps, both of the entire ocean, and of each of our 'seven seas'.

Leaving Greenwich our imaginary craft, 'The Seven Seas', laden with poems and illustrations, sails down the Channel to explore the North Atlantic, before entering the Mediterranean Sea at Gibraltar; sailing eastwards we pass through the Suez Canal to reach the Indian Ocean, where we call at various places of interest to the traveller, before arriving at Fremantle in Western Australia; from there we take a circular route round Antarctica to visit ports and islands in the Southern Ocean, before our ship sails around the Cape of Good Hope at the southern tip of Africa to explore the South Atlantic; passing through the Panama Canal, we enter the South Pacific Ocean to see the sights; from there, our ship sails northwards to explore places of interest in the North Pacific; finally, our imaginary voyage takes us as close to the North Pole as a ship may go at present, to encircle the melting northern icecap in the Arctic Ocean, ending with a journey south again through the North Sea (with a brief visit to the Baltic) to end where we began – at Greenwich.

The world-map on the following two pages is designed to enable the reader to follow the imaginary journey of 'The Seven Seas', and see at a glance, the places we have chosen to write about and illustrate – and many more that must await another imaginative voyage – in another book (perhaps).

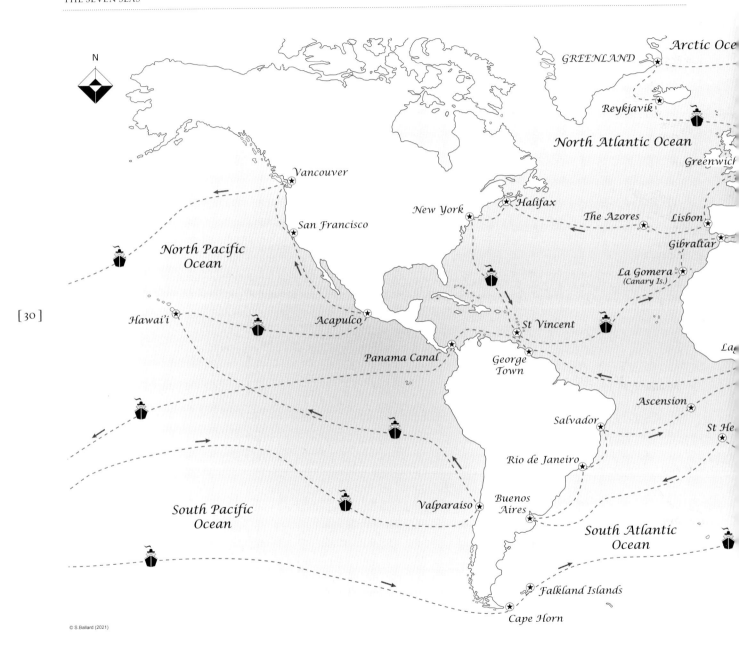

N

GREENLAND

Arctic Oce

Reykjavik

North Atlantic Ocean

Greenwic

Vancouver

New York ★ Halifax

The Azores

Lisbon

Gibraltar

San Francisco

North Pacific
Ocean

La Gomera
(Canary Is.)

[30]

Hawai'i

Acapulco

St Vincent

La

Panama Canal

George
Town

Ascension

St He

Salvador

Rio de Janeiro

South Pacific
Ocean

Valparaiso

Buenos
Aires

South Atlantic
Ocean

Falkland Islands

Cape Horn

© S.Ballard (2021)

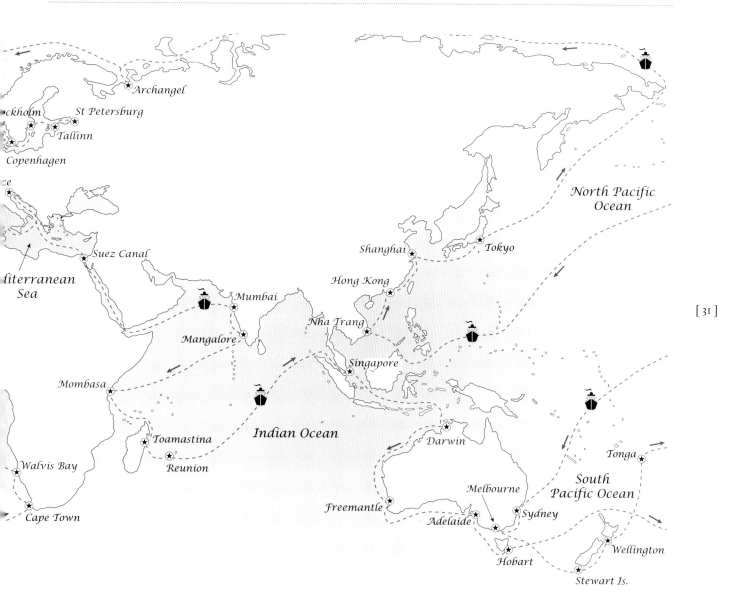

Archangel

Stockholm   St Petersburg

Tallinn

Copenhagen

Mediterranean
Sea

Suez Canal

Mumbai

Mangalore

Mombasa

Toamastina

Walvis Bay

Reunion

Cape Town

Indian Ocean

Nha Trang

Shanghai   Tokyo

Hong Kong

Singapore

Darwin

Freemantle

Adelaide

Melbourne

Sydney

Hobart

Stewart Is.

Wellington

Tonga

South
Pacific Ocean

North Pacific
Ocean

Antarctic Ocean

4. THE CHOICE OF SIGHTS

The stern tyrant Reason wrestles with the wild
shrill anarchy of shameless Feelings.
Only the decent discipline of Choice
allows a happy marriage of mind and heart.

For the sane are mad to imagine they
can trust the fiction of free will, while
madmen are sane in feeling obsessed, compelled...
Insanity's the loss of the illusion of choice.

And yet, I'd rather frame this formal verse
in the affectation of choice, than trust emotion's
anarchy, or reason's rigid tyranny.
Sanity, after all, is an act of faith.

CHOICE IS A SERIOUS BUSINESS. Whether you are choosing a sight to celebrate in paint and verse, or a partner in an enterprise like the creation of this book, or a spouse for life – you need to bring three guides to help you: your head, your heart and time. Good choices usually require 'three green lights': they should be thoughtful, they should feel right, and they should be carefully considered. Those who fall headlong in love are well advised to adopt the discipline of a long(ish) engagement. We did! – well, at least six months...

Likewise, in the making of this book, we have spent many months, not only assuring ourselves of the strength and resilience of the partnership between painter and poet, but also debating the choice of sights to include – and omit. We agreed to adopt the 'three green light' rule – with the added safeguard that two heads (and two hearts) are better than one. As a result, this book has been slow to mature to a state of readiness for publication, and the attention of a critical readership. We believe – and hope you will agree – that it is better for it.

In the event, we have made an eclectic choice of sights – by which we mean that personal preference, rather than rhyme or reason, has guided us in choosing what to include, write verses about, and illustrate – and what to set aside for a possible second volume in the future. Of course, the poet has chosen places, and views, that stimulate and inspire his rhymes, and the artist has her reasons – not least the opportunity for access, since visual art requires the presence of the artist at the location, while poets, who dwell in a world of imagination, can just make things up – with the aid of the internet!

[33]

We are both seasoned travellers, cruise-lecturers, and teachers of the arts of painting and verse. We have been spoilt for choice. Many lovely illustrations, and a few decent poems, have had to be set aside to make the book fit our publisher's prescription ('balanced, not overlong, interesting – and leaving the reader wanting more'). We hope the reader will feel that we have met that brief.

5. THE POEMS

What lasts? — the reasoned thought, not the inventor;
we mark the good advice, but not the mentor;
the justified dissent, not the dissenter;
the tragic news, forgetting the presenter,
                    my friend.

What lasts? — the pyramids, but not the culture:
who cares about old customs of sepulture?
If you pretend a passion for the occult, you're
revealed as just another culture-vulture,
                    my dear!

What lasts? — the artefacts, but not the makers.
Their pains will perish with the poor pains-takers.
Those craftsmen aren't time's movers or time's shakers —
it's craftsmanship creates ageless heart-breakers,
                    that's clear.

What lasts? — the poetry, not grief nor pleasure;
(making good verse is more like work than leisure;)
each must appeal, the message and the measure.
Write something, if you seek enduring treasure
                    right here.

Art lasts, the crafts endure, and architecture,
ideas, invention, science and conjecture.
The lecturer's forgotten, not the lecture.
So — speak immortal words, when you expect your
                    life's end.

THE ART OR CRAFT OF POETRY HAS FROM THE START OF OUR HISTORY engaged and fascinated speakers of English and literary people, both authors and readers. English poetry (or, better poetry in English) is one of the gre atest glories of our culture: today it is practised, read and studied worldwide. Our earliest surviving poem (Caedmon's Hymn) was composed towards the end of the 8th century in Northumbria (then the cultural centre of Britain, and possibly of Europe) more than a millennium ago. In that time we may discern three ages (or stages) of poetry: the Old English alliterative tradition (*Beowulf* to Langland's *Piers Plowman*, 8th-14th centuries), formal syllable-measured and (mostly) rhymed verse (Chaucer to the Victorians, 14th-19th centuries), and modern verse (20th century –?).

Other arts, like music and painting, show a similar tripartite process of growth and development in the West. Harmony and counterpoint were added to the repertoire of composers and performers in the 15th century, and rapidly displaced the old monophonic style of early music. And the advent of 20th-century modernism led to the creation of atonal music in the work of Schoenberg and others. The discovery of perspective in art brought a quality of almost photographic realism into painting in the Renaissance, while the 20th-century exploration of various kinds of abstract art challenged the very notion of representation and form. In each case the relative simplicity of the medieval artistic forms was developed into ever more complex creative structures, like the sestina or sonata or the Last Supper, before the revolution of modernism attempted to sweep away the great traditions of formal verse, tonality in music, and representation in art. (It failed!)

[35]

Anglo-Saxon verse has perplexed scholars, who were conditioned to look for complexity – and who consequently taught generations of puzzled students impossibly complex rules of verse structure, quite failing to answer the question: how did the master-poet teach his young apprentice? In fact, Old English verse can be adequately (and accurately) described by specifying that (apart from occasional poetic licences, like the short (half) line or the extended line) the standard (Caedmonian) line is formed of two half-lines each containing two (no more, no less) stressed syllables and any convenient number of unstressed syllables, arranged at will, and consistent with the demands of the language and meaning, such that most lines (with very few exceptions) have at least eight syllables – and seldom more than twice that number, with alliteration ('front-rhyme') linking the third stressed syllable with either the first or second (or both) – but never with the fourth. Study the sestina forming the Envoi to this book (pp.196-7), which uses a modern version of the Anglo-Saxon line, to understand how this kind of verse is organised, using the first consonant of the alliterating words (with the special rules that initial *st-*, *sp-* and *sc-* (modern *sh-*) are treated as single sounds, and words beginning with a vowel alliterate freely with one another – as if they started with a 'zero consonant') – *with lel letteres loken*, 'linked by matching letters' (i.e. sounds), as one of the very last practitioners of this style (until now) described it – though the ballads and nursery rhymes (popular verse) show the continuity of the 'stress-counting' tradition: 'One, Two, Buckle my shoe...' (I could go on, but the rest is detail!)

Chaucer and his contemporaries (like 'moral' Gower) abandoned the Old English stress-measured verse line in favour of the new continental model of syllable-measured verse, and also replaced front-rhyme (alliteration) with end-rhyme: *Whanne that Aprille with his shoures sote/The droghte of Marche hath perced to the rote...* 'When April comes, bringing its soothing showers/After a dry March to infuse the flowers...' Each line has ten syllables, forming a rhyming couplet. This new style rapidly became normalised; with very few exceptions, all poets adopted it – so that by Shakespeare's time two centuries later, this was how English verse was composed. (Blank verse is rhymeless syllable-counted verse, typically decasyllabic.)

[36] However, it is worth noting that languages fall into two broadly contrasting groups: those that arrange speech by 'syllable-timing' (like French or Italian, which keep an even space of time between each syllable (*Où sont les neiges d'antan?*) and those, like English or German, which employ 'stress-timing' – maintaining an even space of time between each stressed syllable (*Where are the snows of yesteryear?*). The astonishing thing about 'classic English verse' (from Chaucer to Tennyson) is that it employs a sort of counterpoint between the natural stress-timed patterns of the language and the artificial syllable-measured lines into which it is organised. Try reading aloud the first two lines of Shakespeare's sonnet *Let me not to the marriage of true minds/Admit impediments. Love is not love...* to feel the tension between the demands of the language and the measure of the verse. Good poets exploit this feature, which I have called the counterpoint of (classic) English verse.

This great tradition was challenged by the modernist revolution of the 20th century, which taught us to abandon line-initial capital letters (a trivial change) and to write free verse – poetry composed without any metrical structure, where the only evidence that the composition is poetry, not prose, is the failure of the lines, which are separated by neither rhyme nor reason, to ever quite reach the right-hand margin of the printed page. Free verse is formless. Please observe how each of the three great arts, poetry, painting and music, tried to abandon formal structure in the 20th century – and also (as far as possible) meaning, for example in nonsense verse, abstract art, or atonal music.

But although the creators of such 'formless, meaningless' art may feel they have achieved their aims, the creation of a work of art, or literature, or music, is only half of the process of its realisation: the other half is provided by the viewer, reader or audience – who receive, interpret, understand and (one hopes) appreciate the creator's offering. 'Man is a meaning-seeking animal', a wise man once wrote; humans are also conditioned to seek out form and structure, even where there is none intended. Free verse may be formless (and, sometimes, meaningless) for the poet, but readers find shape (and sense) in any arbitrary distribution of words on a page. Free verse is literally a contradiction in terms.

The poems in this book are written to exemplify (in modern English) each of the three stages of English [37] poetry outlined above: for example, the one at the head of this section is 'classic' syllable-measured, rhymed verse, while the one that heads the next section is stress-measured and alliterative in form. Attentive readers may spot one or two experimental forms (the 'sonnet redoublé', for example). Look for the one (or two) examples of apparently free verse, and consider whether they are truly formless. (I hope readers will not find anything I have written meaningless!)

6. THE PAINTINGS

The medium is the message, Marshal McLuhan
told us. The arts are also defined,
distinguished and determined by the constraints of medium.
Music is sound – in melody and harmony;
poetry language – in line and verse.
Painting's medium is paint, of course –
and light and shadow, shape and outline,
(water-colour, crayon, acrylic and oil-paint)
tone and colour, composition,
space and distance, perspective...what else?
Mastering an art means learning how to
master the medium. The medium controls
the craftsman and the artist: descriptive art's
the painter's forte; the poet's a raconteur;
music creates mood and feeling.
Medium is the true *magister artium.*
The medium is the master, he might have said.

SL writes: MY DRIVE TO PAINT STARTED EARLY IN LIFE. As an only child I loved observing and setting down the effects of light and shapes of places and the likenesses of people. Inventing stories, I would always illustrate them. I owe a debt of gratitude to my long-suffering grandmother, who would patiently pose for me for hours at a time.

When I was fortunately offered an opportunity to read English at Oxford and, at the same time, a place at the Ruskin School of Art, I had to make a difficult choice. I chose English, but took my easel with me to the large garret room in St Margaret's Road and St Hugh's College. It was fun to try to illustrate Chaucer's verse with zany cross-eyed horses and caricatures to capture the humour of *The Canterbury Tales.*

For me, the process of creating images has always been a source of pleasure, and as important as the finished work itself: sketching, calligraphy, blending oil paints, scumbling, pastels – with the special joy of letting one colour leech into another (which I call the 'bleeding' loveliness of watercolour...). One year, I was thrilled and privileged to be a winner of the *Sunday Times* Watercolour Competition and, in another, selected for the Summer Exhibition at The Royal Academy. Both of the winning pictures were illustrations of places my husband and I had visited, one of the (rather smelly) dye-vats in Morocco, and the other of an Amazonian Steamer. As one of the artists in the Medici Gallery's 'Summer in the City' exhibition, I grew to love illustrating buildings, as well as the representation of figures, which have since childhood provided the life-blood of my paintings.

[39]

I hope I have been able to do justice to John Elinger's complex, witty and intricate poems. Painting conveys emotion and can create a powerful image, I believe, whereas poetry may take our thoughts to a deeper level and offer a different kind of reward for the attentive reader. Together, and in partnership, we hope you may find something here to delight, inspire and move you.

My love of the arts (in all their forms), but especially painting, is matched only by my love of our family – and, above all, of my husband, John, to whom we have dedicated this book *in memoriam.* (I cannot call him *late,* as he was always on time, or even ahead of it.)

How can one capture a great heart in words or painting?

John had a great heart, a generous spirit, and a loving personality. He was an inspirational teacher of hundreds of students and schoolchildren. He savoured the challenge of lecturing to an audience, not only in Oxford and Cambridge, but also (latterly) on cruise liners – which is where we first met Wendy and Christopher (the poet, John Elinger).

He was a prolific author and historian; beside our family, his books are his legacy. They preserve something of the essence of the man. I was delighted to illustrate several of them, including one on the Bloomsbury Group, and another about Lyme Regis, which had become our much-loved home in recent years.

John was a keen advocate, as I am, of 'enjoying the process' of what one is doing – rather than being for ever hung up on goals and achievements. For him, the 'process' was to live his faith, a staunch Christian faith, and to live in the moment, full of humour and grace. He loved meeting people, enjoyed antiques and collected 19th-century watercolours. A talented pianist and a fine singer, music was key to his zest for life.

The son of a sailor, John had blue sailor's eyes. He was far-sighted in all senses, and had a voice to reach across lecture halls and school assemblies. As a young schoolmaster, he wore metal tips on his shoes to give notice of his arrival – and his footsteps echo in the memory of his pupils. I hope this book might echo his full, and faith-filled, life.

From the start he encouraged us and enthusiastically supported us in the labour of planning, creating and compiling this book of poems and pictures. I recall the day when we first envisaged it, as the four of us watched the sun slowly sink beyond the southern ocean. I know he would want to urge you to enjoy the book, which we have chosen to complete as a memorial for him.

7. AFTERWORD

We shall not all die, though each one must die –
vanish like smoke or empires, feelings or
religions, languages, or days of yore.
Where are those years of youth, the times gone by?
Where Gothic, Hittite, or Etruscan? Why
did men once worship Isis, Zeus and Thor?
All feelings fade; nor grief, nor love endure.
Like Persia, Babylon, or Rome, we die.

And yet, art is immortal. Only art
survives. In music, paintings, poetry,
lost empires, ancient passions, antique faiths,
old tongues – the precious past – revive like wraiths
to live again. Though we and life must part,
art lives: we shall not altogether die.

THE PAINTER AND THE POET WHO MADE THIS BOOK MET ON A CRUISE — but we can't quite remember which one it was, of the many voyages we have made with our partners (in life and work) during the last dozen or so years! We are both 'cruise lecturers' and teachers of the arts of painting and verse on land and sea. Our partners, John and Wendy, have provided back-up, constructive criticism and their own special skills. We thank them both. Wendy managed the IT for me, and (in a white dress) provided a 'woman's voice' for a lecture on Emily Dickinson: she has generously proof-read this volume more than once, as it gradually took shape. John, who sadly did not live to see the publication of our work, gave us advice, encouragement and support from the outset of the project. He would, we feel sure, have offered cogent, kind and perceptive criticism of the several drafts, as we completed them. We sadly miss his presence today: he was a good friend and a very special 'life-partner'. The book is dedicated to his memory.

[43]

We also wish to record our gratitude to our patient publisher, James Ferguson, and the designer of the book, Andrew Esson, and to Sebastian Ballard who provided the splendid maps. We alone are responsible for any errors and infelicities that remain. For better or for worse, the book is finished at last! We hope that those who read it will find it instructive, rewarding and enjoyable.

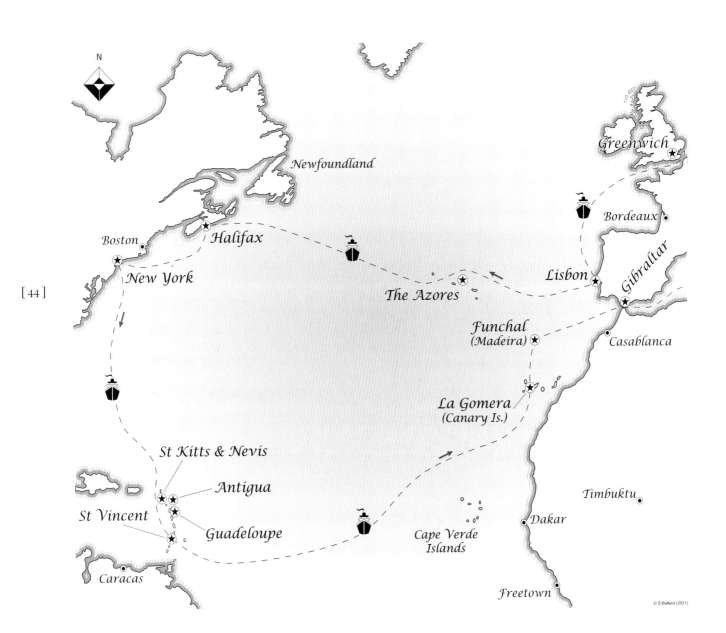

N

Newfoundland

Greenwich

Bordeaux

Boston

Halifax

New York

The Azores

Lisbon

Gibraltar

Funchal
(Madeira)

Casablanca

La Gomera
(Canary Is.)

St Kitts & Nevis

Antigua

St Vincent

Guadeloupe

Timbuktu

Dakar

Caracas

Cape Verde
Islands

Freetown

© S.Ballard (2021)

I. THE NORTH ATLANTIC OCEAN

The sea is never still. Today the waves,
white-feathered, cringe and fawn around the ship,
which flings them back in slabs of foam that slip
beyond the stern to lay the path that paves
the sea behind it. Salt-spray stings, and laves
the deck. The water glitters. Sunlight drip-
dries spattered portholes. Random wavelets dip
and dance in disarray. One fat cloud saves
the sky from uniformity, and drops
a sudden shower, creating in the east
a faint unfinished bow. Seawater slops
and slaps against the ship, which seems to flee
from some mysterious slumbering beast
concealed within this vast unquiet sea.

UNLIKE THE SOUTH ATLANTIC, ITS NORTHERN NEIGHBOUR HAS A DIVERSE COASTLINE, a multitude of islands, and several tributary seas, including the Caribbean, the North Sea and the Baltic, and (of course) the Mediterranean Sea, the watery cradle of our western civilisation. Largely unseen, except by navigational instruments, the Atlantic Ridge which stretches roughly southwards from Iceland, divides the ocean into two vast basins. Islands, such as the Azores and Ascension Island, form the high peaks of this Ridge, which (if the sea was drained away) would emerge as the world's longest mountain range

The Atlantic takes its name from the lost (or mythical?) continent of Atlantis. It is the saltiest of all the oceans, due to the water flowing from the Mediterranean, which has a very high rate of evaporation and relatively low inflow of fresh water. The prevailing wind is from the west. It provides mankind with oil, gas, gravel, and fish.

The inexhaustible demand for what is proving to be an exhaustible supply of edible fish has led to dangerous levels of over-fishing of many species, such as cod. Until the middle of the last century the North Atlantic was the world's busiest sea-route, but air travel and the changing patterns of global trade have somewhat reduced its pre-eminence.

Starting from Greenwich, our imaginary voyage takes us down the English Channel and across the Bay of Biscay to Lisbon. From there we sail westwards to the Azores, crossing the ocean to reach Halifax in Nova Scotia. Turning south, we visit New York and continue towards the Caribbean Sea, calling in at several of the many fascinating islands in that archipelago; from where we set off eastwards, re-crossing the Atlantic and, after dropping anchor briefly in Madeira and the Canary Islands, we arrive at Gibraltar, the gateway to the Mediterranean.

Seawater slops and slaps
against the ship,
which seems to flee from some
mysterious slumbering beast
concealed within this vast unquiet sea.

LISBON

Founded (in fable) by Ulysses – once
'Olispo' – Lisbon is the foremost port
and capital of Portugal, and fronts
the fierce Atlantic breakers like a fort

guarding the western tip of Europe, where
the Tagus meets the sea. Lisbon is built
on several hills, like Rome: visit the Square
with fountains, theatre, and a patchwork quilt

of white and black mosaic tiles. Nearby,
another, known as Black Horse Square, is found
through a triumphal arch. About these lie
churches and palaces. Towers abound

across this City with a history:
founded in fact by the Phoenicians, then
governed by Rome, the Visigoths, set free
at last from Moorish domination when

Crusaders and a month-long siege restored
self-government, allowing this great port
to grow and flourish. (Trade promotes, the sword
destroys, a city's wealth.) Lisbon, in short,

became the portal of an empire, whence
the Spanish fleet (the famed Armada) sailed
to perish on the British shores. (Defence
succeeded, where attempted conquest failed:

aggression's always wrong, and seldom pays.)
The 'oldest allies' now, Britain and Portugal
compete, for nations must, in peaceful ways:
in sport and tourism. Today, with all

the old disasters – earthquakes, hunger, wars
and plague forgotten, sunlit Lisbon thrives
and welcomes visitors from distant shores.
While death's supreme, humanity survives.

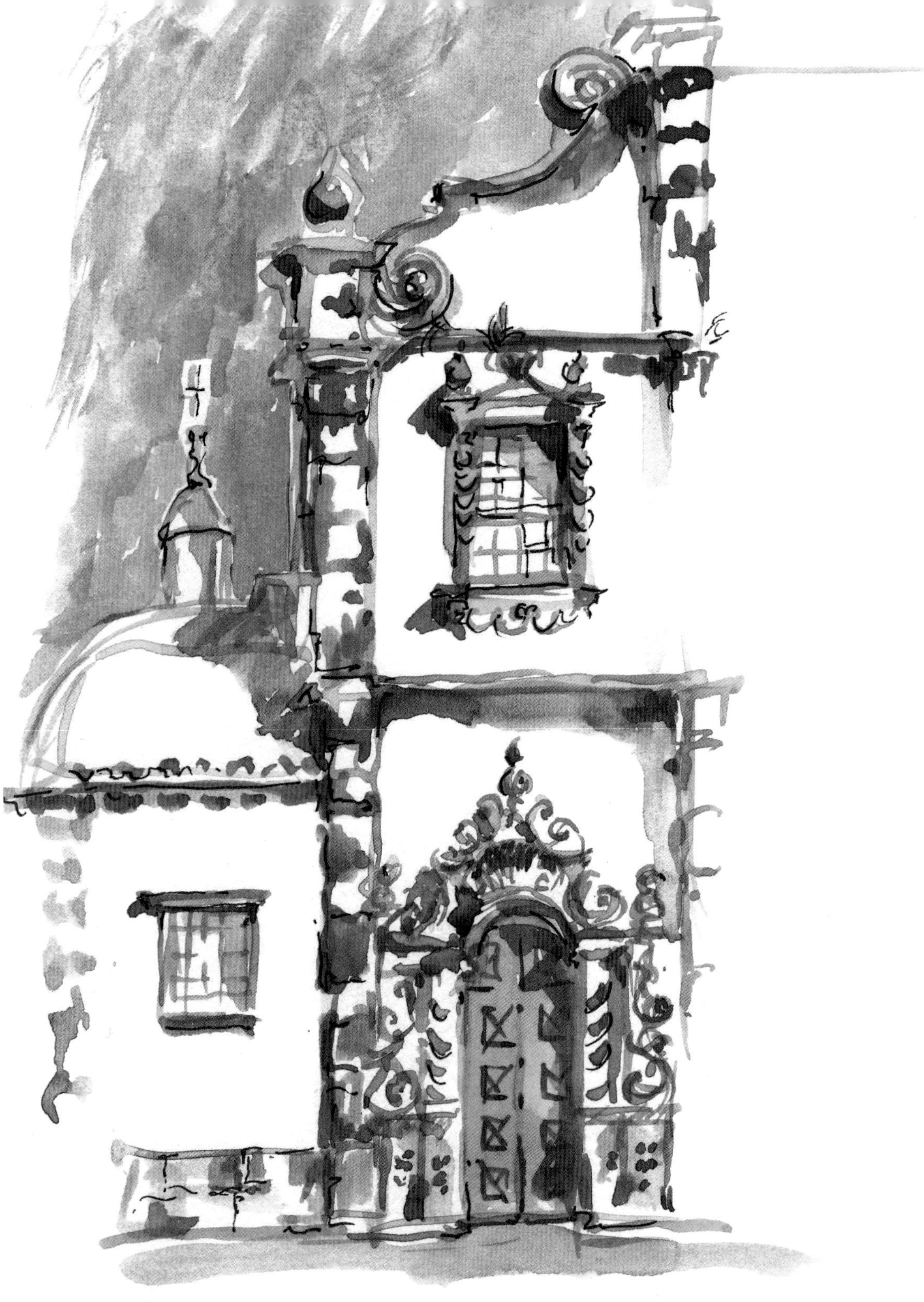

THE AZORES

Midway between three continents appears
the flower-garden of the green Azores.
Sea-surfeited, the mother-ship finds shores
where pineapples and cattle flourish. Here's
a haven, once the clouded weather clears;
here homesick, sea-sick travellers may pause,
and send a postcard home. This place restores
the weary seafarer at last, and cheers
a jaded tourist with good coffee, views
of lakes and churches, basalt and baroque,
and steaming iron-stained fresh springs that spill
warm streams. These isolated islands still
provide a welcome respite from the cruise
for sailors, while the good ship rests in dock.

A few prefer the sea-days, most the ports
where you may walk along the sea-front, take
a trip, or drink a tincture in a bar.
I like them both – but when you come from far
away these islands in the sunlight make
a welcome landfall for the ones whose thoughts
are turning shore-wards and for whom dry land
and stable footing feel like Paradise.
Volcanoes – settlements – then merchandise
provide the framework for the triple-strand
development of these nine islands and
the islets near them. As you lick your ice,
or sip your wine, recall that twice or thrice
they've helped England fight tyrants, and withstand.

[51]

HALIFAX

The capital of Nova Scotia, Halifax,
  home of the Mi'kmaq people once,
  today the friendly 'city of the future',
  was named and settled by the colonists
  in 1749; this led to war,
  inevitably won by European
  superior technology, which made
the capital of Nova Scotia, Halifax.

In 1817 in friendly Halifax
  disaster struck: the largest man-made blast
  before the advent of atomic bombs
  was caused by a collision in 'The Narrows';
  a French munitions-ship exploded near
  the docks; the 'Halifax disaster' left
  nine thousand injured and two thousand dead
in 1817 in friendly Halifax.

Among large cities ranked the leader, Halifax,
  for quality of life today, enjoys
  warm summers and mild winters, courtesy
  of the Gulf Stream. The City's kind to those
  who walk (like me) and wish to see the sights
  and share its culture, learn its history.
  The parks and Broadwalk witness why this is
among large cities ranked the leader, Halifax.

New York*

Here at the sea-washed, sunset gates there stands
A mighty statue, Liberty, whose crown
of seven rays illumes the seven seas,
the seven continents, the circling globe –
a gift from France in 1886,
a decade and a century from when
the Founding Fathers made their Declaration
of Independence on July the Fourth.

Mother of Exiles, from her beacon-hand
Glows world-wide welcome; at her feet there lies
a broken chain, symbol of slavery
and tyranny. The thirst for *Liberté,*
Égalité, Fraternité is shared
by all humanity: while liberty's
essential for a good life, what about
equality – and true companionship?

Give me your tired, your poor, she seems to say,
Your huddled masses, yearning to breathe free.
Today those masses huddle still, and breathe
polluted air; if abject poverty's
reduced, those 'relatively poor' increase
each year, as wealth and envy escalate;
and all the world feels weary and distressed...
another century – and much the same.

I lift my lamp beside the golden door
to freedom – *life, liberty, the pursuit*
of happiness, as Jefferson proclaimed.
Our lives last longer now, our liberty's
secured more widely in the world each year.
But has the sum of human happiness
increased, I wonder...? We should not despair:
it may seem slow, but progress still is sure.

[54]

*This poem takes its inspiration from a sonnet written in 1883 by
the American poet Emma Lazarus in support of the campaign to
raise funds in the USA for the pedestal of the Statue of Liberty,
upon which the well-known lines from the poem are inscribed.*

HMS Roce

ANTIGUA

Warm seas, warm days, warm welcome at St. John's:
steel bands and jolly pirates on the quay.
Tourists emerge, like prisoners set free,
from ships at rest from ocean marathons.

A year of beaches (which one pleased the Queen?) –
twelve miles of history (cannons, forts!) surround
this Leeward Island called Antigua – found,
and named, by Christopher Columbus – green

and golden like an orange-tree in bloom –
to honour 'old St. Mary's' in Seville.
Here everything feels good, and nothing ill –
but here the earliest settlers met their doom.

Lord Nelson's dockyard (now restored) recalls
the age of naval battles and those wars
which France and England fought by distant shores -
where waves break gently now – a sea-bird calls.

Those wars have ceased - and slavery's become
a slowly-fading stain today – but sin
transforms, revives and triumphs in
the scourge of shopping and the stench of rum.

Forget the booze, the gin, the jungle-juice,
the cheap boutique, the trashy souvenir!
Look for the local Post Office – find where
they sold Antigua's fabled 'Penny Puce' –

a small fortune can't buy you one today:
the stamp's unique! Antigua's special too –
and less expensive. So, enjoy the view,
the air (they're free) before you sail away.

Tourists return, like children back at school,
to ships at rest from ocean marathons.
Warm seas, warm days, warm welcome at St. John's,
where folk are friendly and the culture's cool.

[57]

St. Vincent

The capital is Kingstown – start from there:
on Grenville Street, a stone's throw from the Port,
three Christian churches, cheek by jowl, today
compete for congregations and support.
Cultures and faiths, like empires, fracture and decay.

Now climb (or take a taxi) up to where
at Johnson's Point on top of Berkshire Hill
there stands Queen Charlotte's great, forbidding fort,
with cannon pointing inland, trained to kill
the rebel Caribs who, once they were found and caught

(some sins of empire seem beyond repair)
disarmed and hopeless, with their leader dead,
were taken to a rocky island, left
to starve – so trade and slavery could thrive instead...
(Was he so wrong who wrote that property is theft?)

In time, the population learned to share
the wealth that sugar, rum and breadfruit bring –
the colonists, the slaves, their Carib wives.
Social co-operation is the thing
that best yields health, wealth, happiness in people's lives.

To build a brand-new dwelling (or repair
a ruin) here, you call your buddies round
who, in return for grub and rum, will do
the work you need to raise upon the ground
you own, a perfect brightly-painted home for you.

The Public Gardens are beyond compare
for age and interest, with breadfruit brought
by Captain Bligh, St Vincent parrots – blue
and green and gold – reflected, we are taught,
upon the island's flag which proudly flies on view.

A place where hope has now replaced despair
and old suspicion's given way to trust,
St. Vincent is a fertile Paradise:
the weather's kind, the laws today are just...
(the staple exports – arrowroot, bananas, rice).

Islands like this are places where
real progress has proved possible, and may
yet spread worldwide. The visitor who's here
to view exotic sights should go away
amazed – we've seen a better future, worth a cheer.

The Slave Bell
Tower
Romney Mana
St Kitts.

St. Kitts and Nevis

Named by Columbus (for Columbus?) Kitts
recalls the saint who carried Christ across
the raging torrent on his shoulders. Its
history's a fading patchwork quilt of gain and loss.

The Caribs came at first, then Europeans –
who killed two thousand natives in one day.
(Technology's supreme.) The Caribbean's
littered with signs of ancient warfare and affray...

...and slavery. Slaves worked the sugar cane
plantations here, making the owners rich.
Their loss of freedom matched their masters' gain –
the sins of avarice (a constant human itch)

and greed: tobacco, rum give short-lived pleasure
and shorten lives. These 'isles of Paradise'
hold serpents reared to tempt us at our leisure:
volcanoes smoke, and storms may gather in a trice.

The French and English fought to own these isles
of Kitts – and Nevis, nearby southern twin.
Although some names (and food) reflect both styles,
our history books record the British always win.

All empires fail, and fall at last. Today's
new state is free from foreign rule. The slaves
and sugar cane have gone. Tourism pays
better – and fills so many fewer early graves.

Nevis, where Nelson wed, and Hamilton
was born, and Princess Di (and Oprah) stayed
(and many more celebrities) – this is the one
where I would wish to while away my last decade.

For what I most remember is the spray
we felt, crossing the narrow strait, the sun;
the dish of fish we ate for lunch that day;
and smiles, and courtesy and care – and fun.

[61]

GUADELOUPE

This 'Emerald Island' is a butterfly
in shape, with wings – Basse-Terre, Grande-Terre.
It's French. Its population is a mix
of native Caribs, colonists from France,
and slaves brought in to grow the sugar crop.
That's it: the land, the language, and the people.

The Caribs called it Karukera, 'Isle
of Lovely Waters', while *Guadeloupe*
'River of Love' (in Arabic) perhaps
explains why visitors from Britain call
it Paradise, and seek out Sainte-Rose
where *Death in Paradise* is brought to life.

In spite of earthquakes, hurricanes, and fires,
fiction today competes with fact to win
our brief attention: TV's more real than
reality. But what I shall recall's
the palm-tree in the garden up the hill
which flowers after fifty years – then dies.

All fiction lies. In Paradise there was no death –
but in real life, whatever lives must really die.

FUNCHAL

Madeira: woods and wine and waterfalls
from mountains reached by cable-cars, or feet
on perilous levadas – little walls
that hold the water making grapes grow sweet.

Madeira: whales and dolphins dive and weave
the waves. Enchanted by an element
not ours, we watch in wonder, loth to leave
this island of delights and calm content.

Madeira's garden city of the east
Atlantic offers sights to please the eye –
museums, churches, fortress and, not least,
the Workers' Market and the parks nearby.

Madeira welcomes weary seafarers
who, sick for home, have come to understand
the simple pleasures of a port, because –
although we sail the seas, we live on land.

LA GOMERA*

The rainbow, rooted in the sea a mile
away, promising sunken treasure, fades
as the busy ferry approaches in
a fuss of foam. The sea is speckled with
white horses – like flock wallpaper – dark blue
and white beneath a paler sky. And here
the foreground is cactus, palms dancing in
the light wind, and an Indian bean tree bent
like an old man. A solitary pigeon
pecks at the gravel. We sit down to eat.

*La Gomera is one of the smaller, and perhaps the
most attractive, of the Canary Islands.

[67]

GIBRALTAR

'As solid as a rock', Gibraltar is
one half of the Pillars of Hercules
(the other's Mount Abyla to the south)
the limits of the known world once, the mouth
of the Mediterranean today
(the sea where western culture's seed-bed lay
some two or three millennia ago).
Famed for its apes, and galleries below
the surface, castle (relic of the Moors)
actor (and victim) in so many wars,
Gibraltar is disputed territory:
de facto British, claimed by Spain, its story
unfinished yet – although by conquest, choice
and treaty British – wearied by the voice
of politicians, Brexit might persuade
its people that for safety's sake (and trade)
the larger Union should be preferred.
(And which electorate will then have erred?)
While Barbary Apes remain, the British too will stay.
Nature knows best. (At least, I'm told that's what they say!)

[69]

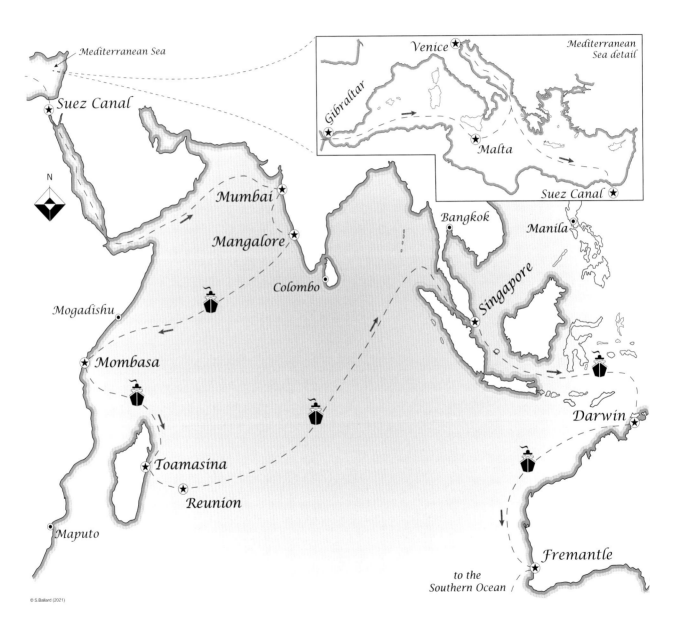

Mediterranean Sea

Suez Canal

Mediterranean
Sea detail

Venice

Gibraltar

Malta

Suez Canal

N

Mumbai

Mangalore

Bangkok

Manila

Colombo

Singapore

Mogadishu

Mombasa

Darwin

Toamasina

Reunion

Maputo

Fremantle

to the
Southern Ocean

[70]

© S.Ballard (2021)

2. The Mediterranean Sea and THE INDIAN OCEAN

The sea is calm, the waves
relent from last night's swell.
A rainbow fades, like hope
of heaven, or fear of hell.

This god-forsaking age
expects no life to come.
Only the best we can
be now, or could become,

inspires mortality.
For death is meaningless:
we die, but – living – fail
to grasp this nothingness

that lies ahead, like rocks
half-hidden, poised to wreck
the unsuspecting ship,
where we recline on deck.

The sea is calm, the waves
relent from last night's swell.
The rainbow fades, like hope
of heaven, or fear of hell.

The Mediterranean Sea is a relic of what was once a mighty ocean, named Tethys, gradually constricted by the continental drift which brought Europe and Africa closer together. It is more than 2,500 miles long, but in places the two continents almost meet (as at the western end). What was an ocean is now a long, winding, narrow waterway. Like the major oceans today, it is divided into a number of minor basins separated by submarine ridges. These contain a floor of brownish sediment, ranging from some 300 to nearly 9,000 feet in thickness, which remain largely undisturbed as a result of the virtual absence of tidal fluctuation except at the western end near Gibraltar. The Mediterranean is sunnier, warmer, and therefore saltier, than the Atlantic Ocean, due to more intense evaporation. The surface currents flow in an anti-clockwise direction. The sea has a number of distinct wind-systems, like the sirocco blowing northwards from Africa, or the mistral of southern France.

The Mediterranean is often called 'a melting pot of peoples and cultures'. Around its shores human settlements made many of the great early advances of civilisation, such as agriculture, writing and the wheel. The sea provided a means of communication, commerce and trade – as well as aggression, as successive naval super-powers strove for supremacy. The opening of the Suez Canal in 1869 re-emphasised its importance, after the discovery of the sea-route to the east around the Cape of Good Hope in the 15th century had somewhat eclipsed it. From the 18th to the 20th centuries Britain secured control of the sea (and the Canal), but that era ended with the Suez fiasco of 1956.

Today, more than 100 million people live close to the shores of the Mediterranean, and it is threatened by rising levels of pollution. Nonetheless, its greatest natural resources are the kindly climate, warm sea and extensive beaches: it provides more than half of the world's income from tourism.

The Indian Ocean is more than 6,000 miles wide at its southern boundary with the Antarctic Ocean, but narrows to the north where India and Sri Lanka make a division between the Arabian Sea and the Bay of Bengal. With an area of over 25 million square miles, it is nonetheless smaller than the (undivided) Pacific and Atlantic Oceans. It incorporates two adjacent seas, the Red Sea and the Persian Gulf. Fed by a number of mighty rivers, including the Zambezi, the Indus and the Ganges, the Brahmaputra and the Irrawaddy, together with regular tropical monsoons and frequent heavy rainfalls, the salinity of the Indian Ocean is relatively low.

Like the Atlantic, this ocean has a broad ridge stretching deep under the water from India to Antarctica. Like the Mediterranean, it contains several basins to the west of this ridge. Apart from Sri Lanka and Madagascar, there are a number of smaller islands, mostly volcanic, including the Maldives, the Seychelles, Mauritius and Réunion. The weather is often violent, especially in the monsoon season, and tropical storms and hurricanes can be dangerous. The temperature of the sea is warmest in the north (above 20° C) and cools towards the south to a mere 2° C, as the Indian Ocean merges with the Southern Ocean around Antarctica.

Starting at Gibraltar, our voyage continues through the Mediterranean, calling at Malta and Venice (at the head of the Adriatic Sea), before passing through the Suez Canal and the Red Sea to reach the Indian Ocean. Our fragile craft then visits some of the major ports around, and within, this vast expanse of restless water before finding safe haven at Fremantle, the port that serves Perth in Western Australia.

Malta G.C.

The land, the language and the people make
the nation. Malta's a great melting pot,
where speech, location, history, each take
the spoon in turn to stir the tasty stew
of Maltese citizens and polyglot
migrants with curious tourists – me, and you.

Malta's an island city, built upon
three islands of an archipelago
of islets left untilled by those who've gone
to join the most intensely settled place
in Europe, peaceful now – and healthy, though
conquest and plague have shaped this populace.

Phoenicians ruled, then Carthaginians
and Greeks; the Romans conquered Malta; then
the Moors and Normans came – Sicilians
and Spaniards, Knights Hospitaller; the great
Napoleon made Malta French, but when
he lost his massive empire, Malta's fate

depended on another island – ours.
Its naval base controlled 'the middle sea'
and new canal at Suez. Other powers
that threatened Britain's might were kept at bay.
'Nurse of the Med' in World War I – G.C.
awarded in the second great affray.

Malta's proud flag reminds us of those years
when Britain and her allies stood alone
against the common enemy. The tears
and rage of World War II are now replaced
by gentle smiles of welcome, kindness shown
to strangers, tours and treats for every taste.

The island's name, if Greek, means 'honey' – though
Phoenician *maleth* means 'a haven': here's
a land of sanctuary and sweetness. Go
to see the megaliths; imagine once
dwarf elephants roamed here; or drink some beers
and wander by the many waterfronts.

St. Paul was shipwrecked here, though Malta now
has several harbours and safe anchorage
where sightseers may land to study how
this island earns its living: tourism
(for health and recreation), harbourage
for cruise-ships, trade and films – and people come

attracted by the climate and the views,
by Malta's history and geography,
to go ashore after an ocean-cruise,
to see the 'cart-tracks' in eroded rock,
by independence and neutrality,
and other reasons, good, bad – or ad hoc.

The local customs, proverbs, festivals
(like Mnarja), strange and colourful, expose
a hidden life. While births and burials
determine culture, scholars teach us, yet
'A childless marriage can't be happy' shows
us more of Malta than the Internet.

A child's first birthday is a special day:
traditionally, they're placed within a ring
of objects of symbolic value – tray
(service), book (learning), ripe tomato (cook) …
Their path in life is signalled by the thing
they turn towards. (I guess I chose the book!)

The languages of Malta are Maltese
and English, though Italian's often heard
(and many others brought by migrants): these
three languages competed to be made
'official' until Parliament preferred
Maltese and English. Warfare's accolade

is granted only to the victors. Those
who lose, lose everything, their lives, their lands,
even their languages. Whoever goes
through life untouched by war is fortunate.
Who studies Malta's story understands
that peace and freedom are prerequisite.

VENEZIA

Venice I love – *La Serenissima!*
City of water, history and light,
Black gondolas on dark canals and bright-
Painted palaces slowly crumbling. Far
Away across the sea, *Italia*
Pretends to ownership, but the delight
Of Venice is for everyone – a sight
To raise the human spirit, and a star
Among the cities of the world, a sign
That man can make a thing of beauty and
Not spoil it – though it must decay – design
A treasure and not lose it, build by hand
A wonder unsurpassed in any land:
This loveliest city – loveliest in decline!

And now this city may be yours, or mine,
To marvel at and love; San Marco and
The Arsenale, seascapes or the Grand
Canal, sea-smells to spice good food and wine
In *trattorie*, bridges where you stand
In awe that anything should be so fine –
And man-made. Nature's green with envy: are
These rising floods not natural acts of spite
Against a city which reveals the height
Of human art and craftsmanship? The car
Is banished here, but moth and rust still mar
These works of man – with rot and must and blight.
La Fenice revives, but Venice might
Be sinking. Look! The jealous sea's not far...

Canal Crossing Suez
Sander Lello.

THE SUEZ CANAL

The project to create a ship-canal
to link the Red Sea to the Med required
some four millennia and repeated trial
and error from conception to completion
(at twice the promised cost) in 1869.

The Kings of Persia first decreed: 'There shall
be built a waterway...' Venice desired,
Napoleon proposed, to join the Nile
to the Red Sea: the timeless sand's accretion
has long concealed from view each flawed and failed
design.

At last, de Lesseps chose the natural
land-route (Port Said to Suez) and acquired
permission, funds and work-force – all the while
opposed by Britain – we called it 'a Grecian
gift' – Robert Stevenson had built the railway-line!

Disraeli, Rothschilds, and diplomacy
soon gained control of this new passage-way
from east to west, that saved 4,000 miles,
but led to conflict in the years to come:
from World War II's fierce-fought North Africa
campaign,

the Suez crisis (farce or tragedy?)
to the Israeli-Arab wars (are they
yet done?). Only forgiveness reconciles
opponents, but opposing powers become
entrenched in enmity – and sadly there remain

unless our fragile hope for peace can free
us from the treasured wrongs of yesterday.
Meanwhile, the ice melts when the summer smiles
along the north-east passage, saving some
more thousand miles ... to render the Canal in vain?

MUMBAI

A melting pot of many cultures –
old Bombay, new Bollywood –
once a Queen's dowry, now capital of the State
of Maharashtra, the commercial and financial
capital of India, an 'island city',
first occupied by fishermen,
governed by several successive dynasties
until the Mogul Empire permitted the Portuguese
to take control in the Treaty of Bassein
in 1534, and fortify the city.
When Catherine of Braganza married the King of England,
Charles II, the seven islands
which form Bombay (Mumbai) became
British, and the city grew in size and wealth.
India became independent
in 1947: the renamed Mumbai
continued to grow greater and wealthier,
and later became the capital city
of Maharashtra, the Marathi-speaking
state partitioned from the State of Gujarat.
Mumbai, at first a fishing village,
later transformed into a colonial centre
of trade and commerce, has become today
the largest city in southern Asia,
the industrial home of Hindu film-making –
and still a melting pot of many cultures.

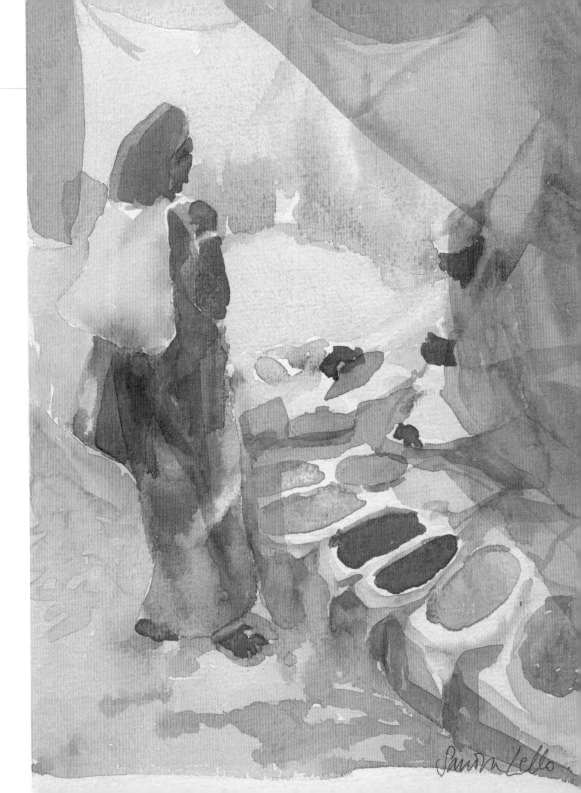

MANGALORE*

'Jewellers since 1935' –
the signs read, proudly.
And I consider
what else significant
has occurred since that time.
Air travel? The pursuit
of European union
(one way or another)?
Television? T-shirts
with memorable messages...
We visited a factory
where they roasted, shelled
and packed the cashew nuts.
Women's work, I noticed:
progress in manufacture

means men first, then women,
and finally machines.
We saw six temples
('One caste, one religion, one God'),
and the Catholic church
of St. Aloysius.
(Superstition is
a global pandemic.)
But who are the more deceived,
the priests, the prayerful,
the pilgrims – or the tourists
accoutred with cameras,
and casual curiosity?
I also since 1935
have sought for the wisdom
worth more than rubies.

[83]

*On the west coast of India, south of Mumbai.

MOMBASA

Mombasa has a troubled history
(the local name means 'strife'): the Portuguese
and Arabs struggled for supremacy,
until the British gained it (by degrees)
and briefly made it Kenya's capital.

Mombasa's rich in contrast – old and new.
Historic harbour beside modern port.
Fort Jesus (once a prison)'s worth a view –
cathedrals, mosques and temples which one ought
to visit (though the past can quickly pall).

Mombasa is a market-city for
the local produce – coffee, cotton, rice
and much besides – built on an isle offshore.
Bridges and busy ferries just suffice
to link the island with the mainland sprawl.

Mombasa is a rail-head for the east
of Africa; the nearby airport makes
the city a key transport-hub, not least
for tourists, as for trade, and links the Lakes
of central Africa with one and all.

Mombasa was where Karen Blixen stayed,
Vasco da Gama came; where music may
be heard all day, all night, and music's made
in many styles; where unemployment's way
above the norm – and will it ever fall?

TOAMASINA (TAMATAVE)

Tree-lined avenues, street-markets, beaches –
beautiful, but sadly much polluted
and patrolled by sharks of all descriptions:
Toamasina is Madagascar's
major port. It's built on sand and coral –
once controlled by France, exporting gold dust
(and the plague) – the 1927
hurricane destroyed it – now rebuilt, a
modern city and the island's trading
and commercial centre – coffee, pepper
and vanilla are among its exports.
Though its fauna are unique – the lemurs
geckos, aye-ayes, crocodiles and bird-life,
with a university and airport,
Tamatave today's the second city
within Malagasy's new Republic –
searching for the secrets of real progress,
education and stability, more
equal distribution of their blessings –
health and wealth and happiness shared fairly.

Réunion

Ici on parle français, on paie avec
Euros, on pense en français – not the French
of Paris, but the local Creole. Here,
the culture's creole, cooking creole, speech
an interesting form of French Creole –
a fusion of the native patois with
the language of the ruling colonists.
Réunion: on vient voir, on va plus sage.

English, like French, has spawned its share of creoles –
but Middle English was the first French Creole!
I like the way that languages converge
(although divergence is more common). When
they do, the speech-sounds merge, the grammar seems
drastically simplified, vocabularies
promiscuously pruned and reassigned.
Réunion's Creole (just like its name)'s unique.

Réunion's a creole island – speech
and customs, culture and cuisine – a world
in microcosm, where we all might learn
what true civilisation really means:
shun what divides, admire distinctiveness –
temples and churches, doctrines, slavery;
volcanoes and vanilla, sugar, smiles.
Reunion: so much to see, so much to learn.

My sister asked me once if what I dreamed
of was 'a khaki world': I'd rather say
'a creole cosmos' – one shared culture, one
language, one nation, one united people,
among the flame-trees and the waterfalls,
freedom, equality, community,
(the formula we learned first from La France)
humanity's eventual reunion.

Flame Tree
Reunion

SINGAPORE

Why can't we all be more like Singapore?
Once a Crown Colony; invaded by Japan,
and occupied; gained independence, chose
to join Malaysia's Federation; then
seceded as a sovereign state at last.
An 'economic tiger' built on skill,
with neither natural resources, nor
surrounding territories, Singapore's
success derives from trade. With no more than
fifty square miles of land – one island, lots
of islets – ranking high in all the lists
of honour (best airport, best port), this is
the smartest, safest city in the world,
a global star of commerce and finance,
which understands (and turns) the keys
of economic progress: first, free trade,
low interest rates, deregulation, and
a first-class infrastructure (technical
and social)... but, those are the easy bits!
What's next? A world-class workforce which
is highly skilled, well-motivated, and
comparatively cheap: I see you wince!
These are the seven secrets of success.
Why can't we all be more like Singapore?

The answer lies in culture, not in schools,
though education here is world-class too.
What works? A culture fostering these three
great virtues: strong, supportive families –
with self-reliant individuals – who
both welcome and adopt the discipline
of lifelong learning. Nothing more, or less,
is requisite for good societies
with health, and wealth, and happiness for all.
Think of these things as you admire the sights,
the parks and gardens, harbour, tree-lined streets
of Singapore, the 'Lion City', and
consider how complacent westerners
might one day learn some wisdom from the east...

DARWIN

After the rainbow rain-clouds gather.
A lightning storm illuminates the city
at sundown. One white yacht appears
and disappears in a sudden deluge of warm rain.
We eat our dinner to the distant sound
of thunder – and remember the mighty typhoon
that crushed the cathedral, and killed so many.

FREMANTLE: THE ROUND HOUSE

Yes, I remember Fremantle –
Freo's the local name – and I
recall the broad Swan River well,
but, most of all, the prisons. Why?

Stone, convict-built, twelve-sided, now
a tourist-trap – this place was where
bad men who mocked what laws allow
were mured in durance and despair.

The Maritime Museum, near
the dock, recounts the histories
of wrecks along the coastline here.
Today, our new technologies –

radar and sonar and the rest –
make sea-ways safe for voyagers.
The ocean's not so fierce a test
of seamanship, as once it was.

Science outstrips society
in progress. Years ago a youth
was duly hanged for villainy
in this old prison. But, the truth

is, even now, we don't know what
to do with young offenders: lock
them up, and leave them there to rot? –
No good – no more's the 'short, sharp shock'.

Love works – and nothing else will do
the trick of reformation for
the ones who err. These walls you view
will never make our world secure.

The modern prison up the hill's
a Youth Hostel today: it's right
it's designated Fremantle's
'distinctive world-heritage site'.

Castle: The Round House

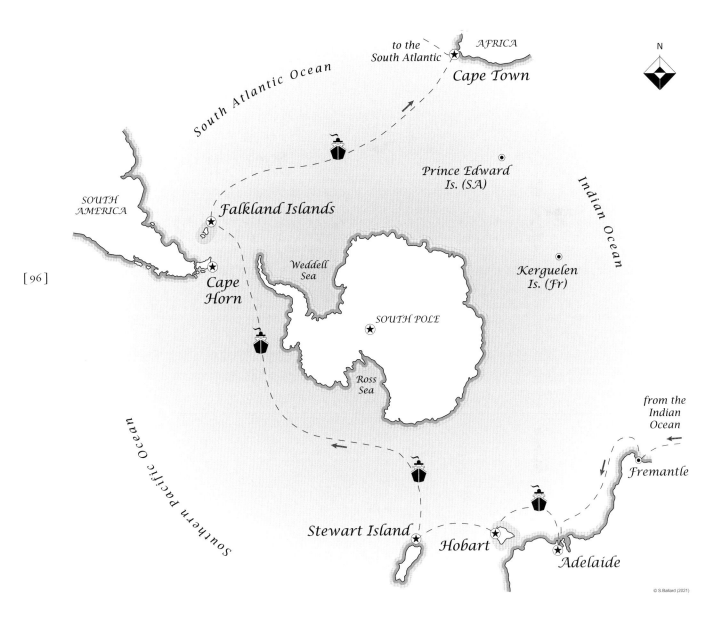

to the
South Atlantic

AFRICA

Cape Town

South Atlantic Ocean

Prince Edward
Is. (SA)

SOUTH
AMERICA

Falkland Islands

Indian Ocean

Weddell
Sea

Kerguelen
Is. (Fr)

Cape
Horn

SOUTH POLE

Ross
Sea

from the
Indian
Ocean

Fremantle

Southern Pacific Ocean

Stewart Island

Hobart

Adelaide

N

[96]

© S.Ballard (2021)

3. THE SOUTHERN OCEAN

ICE-SCULPTURE

'I practise it,' he says, 'for fourteen years'.
The shards and fragments from the block of ice
scatter across the deck like wasted rice
spilt from a punctured bag. His chisel shears
another lump. The emergent shape appears
of some rough beast, a wolf or bear. Each slice
and cut reveals more art – and in a trice
the figure's made, and starts to weep cold tears.
Its life so short – his skill so long to learn!
This is performance-craft: the product dies
as soon as it is born. Before the day
is ended it will melt, and all that beauty turn
to water, disappearing as it dries –
to leave a perfect emblem of decay.

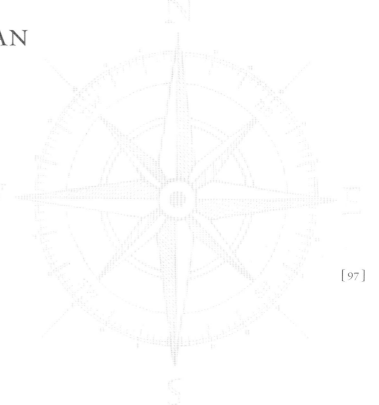

ANTARCTICA IS A CONTINENT, SHAPED RATHER LIKE A DUCK WITH A TWISTED BEAK, entirely covered in ice and more or less inaccessible to tourists. If one could strip away its blanket of ice (as global warming may yet achieve!), it would become apparent that much of the 'continent' lies below sea-level. Antarctica would be revealed as more of an archipelago of islands than a continental mass. It is surrounded by the waters of the Southern Ocean, which merge imperceptibly with the southernmost expanses of the three 'great oceans' – Indian, Atlantic and Pacific.

Indeed, it is difficult to identify the boundary and shape of the Antarctic Ocean, though one might suggest that, when the mean sea-temperature drops below 2° C on a southwards voyage, an 'ocean-boundary' has been crossed. The (British) Admiralty defines the Southern Ocean as the seas below the latitude of 55° S. For the convenience of this book, we are taking a more generous view of the Southern Ocean to allow it to include the waters that border the south coast of Australian and southern tip of New Zealand, together with the Cape of Good Hope and Cape Horn which form the southernmost parts of Africa and South America respectively.

Much of the Antarctic Ocean is ice: in winter the continent doubles in size as the ice-shelf stretches northward into the sea on all sides. A variety of species of whales, seals and fish are found in the Southern Ocean, which provides a habitat for distinctive wildlife such as the penguins. The Antarctic Treaty of 1961 protects the area from exploitation and national rivalry, ensuring that it is preserved for scientific research (and that the penguins are undisturbed). Apart from South Georgia and the Sandwich Islands, the Ocean is not richly endowed with islands, discounting the area hidden beneath the ice-cap. It contains four massive basins reaching depths of three to five miles.

[98]

Our voyage around Antarctica starts at Fremantle in Western Australia and proceeds eastwards along the south coast of that continent, calling at Adelaide, Hobart and Stewart Island (the southernmost point of New Zealand), before reaching the rigours of Drake's Passage and Cape Horn, visiting the Falkland Islands and crossing the South Atlantic (or northernmost extension of the Southern Ocean) to reach the Cape of Good Hope at the southern tip of Africa and finding safe haven in the port of Cape Town.

ADELAIDE

I wonder – would she welcome this memorial,
the faithful wife of the fourth William, Adelaide –
this distant city near the southern ocean, call
it some ten thousand miles from where her bones are laid?

I guess she might – the welcome's warm, the coffee's great,
the streets are wide and clean, and strangely traffic-free;
free buses loop the centre – no one needs to wait
for long; pedestrians may cross diagonally!

[100] And several malls are closed to cars, so visitors
may view the sights unhampered: central Adelaide –
a city packed with parks and churches, as well as
museums, galleries and public buildings – laid

out neatly on a grid of little more than two
square miles of well-planned streets surrounded by
parkland, the river to the north. I doubt that you
can find one better-planned, however hard you try.

And yet, I wonder if the name will really do.
Consider Ayer House: Sir Henry's name today
has been removed from that great Rock called Uluru.
In p.c. Oz, can *Adelaide* be here to stay?

Ayer's House
Adelaide.

HOBART

The natives and the tigers disappeared.
The criminals reformed. The cruel jails
are tourist-traps today. What works is trade –
and tourism. (Buy something!) All else fails.

There's lots to see in Hobart – harbour, malls
with buildings old and new, the gardens, parks
and country-side, Mount Wellington ... and taste
the local beer – before one re-embarks.

Besides the tourists, fish and trees and wool
pass through this port – which gives safe anchorage
to ocean liners and the fishing fleet –
from where one may admire the Derwent Bridge.

The law of life (prosperity for some
means poverty for others) rules the earth
intra- and inter-species: so, beware
mankind's success, which one day won't be worth

a farthing, when we find we have destroyed
the natural environment we need
to live. The tigers of Tasmania
won't be the last to die from human greed.

We visited the Cenotaph: the view
of Hobart is sublime – less so, the thought
of two World Wars, where men from distant lands
came north to serve, and perished as they fought.

Cenotaph Hobart

STEWART ISLAND

Minipopulous, polyonamous*
Stewart Island – 'the storm anchor
of Maui's Canoe'. The Maoris call it
Rakiura, a reference to the light
of 'glowing skies', the glorious sunsets
or the Southern Aurora – visible from South Cape
(the name Captain Cook first gave it);
then New Leinster and New Munster
(provincial names that never caught on)
included the island; an adjunct to Otago
for a time – today the Treaty Settlement
has established its name as Stewart Island/
Rakiura, rather a mouthful

for its small permanent population
of somewhat fewer than 400
souls – and sea-birds: a safe haven
for wild-life, kiwis and kakapo,
a parrot, and trees like podocarps,
the southern conifer. Claiming a right
to independence, the islanders printed
their own passports and postage stamps,
and flew the flag of their future republic
in 1970: now, we might cheer
this minipopulous, polyonamous
island sanctuary – with a sense of humour!

[105]

*Few inhabitants – but a multitude of names!

Antarctica

Among the Seven Seas lie seven continents:
Europe and Asia, Africa, with North and South
America; then Oceania; the last
is called Antarctica, a continent of ice,
far out of sight and mind. It mostly lies beneath
sea-level – and an eiderdown of ice – with no
human inhabitants, unless you count the ones
who come to study penguins, or the polar ice
melting away, as a result of climate change.
Few tourists ever see it, even fewer land
upon this last, lost, lifeless continent of earth.
Although it might be slowly vanishing today,
it may yet prove to be the shape of things to come –
a frozen desert without life, Antarctica.

CAPE HORN

Cape Horn's a headland at the south extreme
of the Tierra del Fuego group
of islands, where two mighty oceans meet.
Drake's Passage links Atlantic and Pacific –
with waves, titanic like the Atlas Mountains,
but rarely peaceful, in this 'sailors' graveyard',
where 'landsmen dream of ship-wreck, peril, death…'
wrote Darwin, and the winds (called *williwaws*)
are treacherous. Rogue waves and icebergs, fierce
currents and gales, that flow and blow, unchecked
by land, unceasingly disturb these seas.
The elements combine to make Cape Horn
the 'Everest' of challenges for ships
and sailors – who, if they survived, would sport
a gold ring in their left ear, and eat dinner
with one foot on the table! After some
two centuries of service as a gateway
between the west and east, the Panama
Canal in 1914 took its place,
and rendered it redundant for all ships
save super-tankers – and the rash-brave ones
who single-handed sail the seven seas.*

[109]

Like Ellen MacArthur.

LIFE CLASS IN THE FALKLANDS

She taught the children how to paint the sea
and sky. A shower of shrapnel killed her, as
she left the safe cocoon of mattresses
to make some coffee for the family.
Her body sprawled across the kitchen floor –
a waste? a sacrifice? a work of art?
a picture – or a lesson – or just dirt
to be cleaned up? A casualty of war.
All human life is meaningless, and so
is death. Occasionally a tourist sees
her name on the Memorial: he's told
she's still remembered in a painting prize
awarded annually, and by the child
who went without her biscuit long ago.

Port Stanley
Falklands

Table Mountain S.A.

CAPE TOWN

A table-cloth of cloud lay spread along
the top of Table Mountain. Down below,
Cape Town was smiling through teardrops of rain.
We saw the fort – the Castle of Good Hope,
the old Company's Garden, the Museum,
statues of Rhodes and Smuts, Mandela, Tutu,
and from the crest of Signal Hill enjoyed
the views of Table Bay and Robben Island...
The story of South Africa – 'a world
in one country' – is not completed yet,
this rainbow nation, with a white and red
lighthouse beside the water's edge, and cranes
along the Waterfront, striped red and white,
like giant statuesque flamingos in the sunlight.

Cape Town's the capital, and westernised:
go north and east to find an Africa
of native cultures and exotic wildlife,
where modern man's not (yet) the master-race.
But even here the rhino, still not quite
extinct, is celebrated by the sea-shore
in art – which can't compete with market-forces.
Getting and spending, we destroy the world
of nature, decimate the species, both
of plants and animals, and foul the nest
for future generations yet unborn.
Cities like Cape Town grow without restraint,
breed crime and poverty and ignorance...
Where is the progress the Enlightenment once
promised?

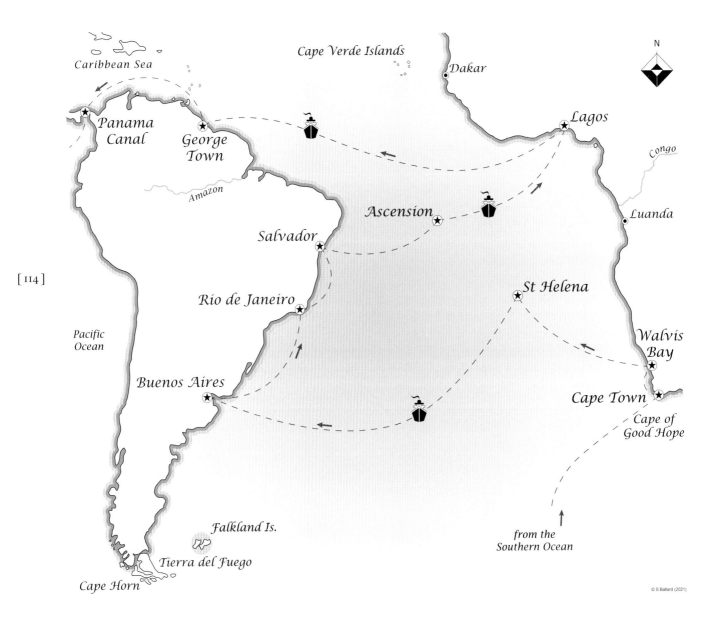

4. THE SOUTH ATLANTIC OCEAN

LA MER
(A translation of the words of the song made famous by Charles Trenet)

The sea –
you see her dance along translucent shores
like silvered glass.
The sea,
reflections shifting
beneath the showers

The sea
and summer skies transform
the white-tipped waves –
angels of purity –
our mother-sea of blue infinity.

Now see
beside the pools
those piles of wet sea-reed,
and see
those white sea-birds,
those buildings showing rust.

The sea
has solaced them
beside translucent bays,
and with her serenade,
life-long, has soothed my soul.

The South Atlantic Ocean contrasts with its northern partner in having a relative lack of islands, tributary seas or variety of coastline. It is more uniform in nature. Both north and south are well supplied with mighty tributary rivers, including the Mississippi, the Amazon and the Niger. Indeed, it is estimated that the Atlantic (north and south) drains a land-area almost four times larger than that supplying either the Pacific (north and south) or the Indian Oceans. The Atlantic is the youngest of the great oceans: it was created when the massive continents of the eastern and western hemispheres began to drift apart, some 180 million years ago. The sinuous South Atlantic, seeming to snake between Africa and South America, reveals to this day how those separate continents must once have fitted together like two halves of a mighty jigsaw puzzle.

St. Helena and Ascension Island are among the few notable islands in the South Atlantic, since we have arbitrarily placed the Falklands Islands in the Antarctic. The submerged Atlantic Ridge, originating a little south of Iceland, continues southwards in an S-shape, consistent with the shape of the Ocean, across the equator to a latitude similar to those of the southern tips of Africa and South America, creating a number of deep basins on either side.

Our voyage, starting from Cape Town in South Africa, proceeds westwards and northwards along the coast of Africa to Walvis Bay in Namibia. We then sail across the ocean, visiting St. Helena as we pass, before exploring the major ports on the eastern side of South America: Buenos Aires, Rio de Janeiro and Salvador. From there we re-cross the South Atlantic, calling at Ascension Island, before reaching Lagos in Nigeria. Finally, we cross the ocean for a third time, north of the equator, to reach Georgetown in Guyana, from where we proceed through the Panama Canal to enter the Pacific Ocean – and the next section of this book.

The sea –
you see her dance
along translucent shores
like silvered glass.

WALVIS BAY

Since Walvis Bay was once called 'whale-fish bay',
we'd hoped to view a whale or two, and fish.
But all we saw was sand – which made us wish
it wasn't there, or might just blow away!
The desert and the dunes are here to stay.
The dunes and desert, brown and yellowish
and dun, display the shells of cuttlefish,
the bones of birds and beasts in slow decay.
The sands and sea, from whence came life, and where
all life returns, are womb and tomb for plants
and animals that haunt the earth, the air
and waters of our precious planet. Chance
and change have shaped these habitats we share,
these lands and oceans of our occupance.

Nature is finest at its most extreme –
the polar ice-caps or the mountain-peaks.
Nothing in art or architecture speaks
so tellingly as that first, faint, slow gleam
of dawn, extinguishing the stars... the streaks
of sunset in the west. Forget your dream
of glory – study nature. Understand
the intricate ecology of life
and landscape – what can best survive the strife
of competition for resources and
shelter in this most harsh and hostile land,
where sun and wind can wound you like a knife,
where water's scarce, and thorn-trees thrive, and life
is brief. What lasts is sea, the sky, and sand.

alvis Bay
Namimbia

John
Lello.

St. Helena

Step from the tender to the quayside.
Walk past the taxis and the vendors –
Cliffs to your left, boats on the sea-side.
Avoid the crowds of careless spenders
      Intent on buying.

First you must honour all the war-dead.
The plain memorial's worth a visit.
Wars achieve little – but make more dead –
You might reflect. Just listen: is it
      A seagull crying?

An archway leads to Jamestown's single
Street and Post Office – send a parcel
Or postcard home now. You can mingle
With locals here. Or view the castle,
      With ensign flying.

The charming church is cool and quiet.
Notice the little painted prison.
I doubt there's ever been a riot!
What need for it could have arisen:
      Desertion, spying?

Nearby, a man-made marvel beckons:
This Jacob's Ladder's a great beacon.
You reach the base in a few seconds –
Ages before you reach the peak, and
      The sweat starts drying!

Climbers who triumph all expect to
Enjoy the view. Your aim and only
Purpose now is to pay respect to
The memory of an Emperor, lonely,
      Deposed and dying.

Rio de Janeiro

Rio de Janeiro

City of contrast: carnival and crime,
Copacabana Beach – Christ, the Redeemer;
city of culture – City of the Arts;
of sport – the Maracana Stadium;
of dance – the Bossa nova, Sambodromo.
Rio was once the capital of both
Brazil and Portugal! – but now, of neither.
Sugarloaf Mountain, reached by cable-car,
provides a view: the harbour, city, slums...
where social inequality prevails,

although diversities, of faith, or race,
or sexual choice, are tolerated here,
where millions, dressed in white each New Year's Eve,
gather to celebrate with chilled champagne:
city of contrast – Rio de Janeiro.
[I wonder why they don't adopt 'the rule
of seven': no one may receive more pay
than seven times the lowest paid employee,
in any enterprise. A rule like this
would soon change social inequality!]*

[123]

We might try it out in the UK first, starting with the Charitable Sector, then (a year later) extending it to the Public Sector (including the universities!), and a year after that introducing it to the Private Sector. We would soon find out how many of our leading lights are more greatly motivated by financial reward, than a desire to serve others. The 'living wage' (in the UK) stands at about £15,000 a year: no one needs more than £105,000 to live well. (Or, if that seems too severe, make it 'the rule of eight, or nine'. Poets, wrote Shelley, are – or they should be – 'the unacknowledged legislators' of the world.) And, of course, this needs to be a global initiative, if it is ever to become fully effective.

ASCENSION ISLAND

Discovered on Ascension Day in May,
1501, Ascension Island lay
unclaimed until the British Crown (concerned
about Napoleon's security
on St. Helena, many miles away)
made it a 'stone frigate' with the Marines
on guard. An 'open prison' in the sea
(for crimes of sodomy and piracy)
from time to time, in recent years it's earned
a living by exporting postage stamps,
and as a military base, with camps,
an airfield, Wideawake (or so I've learned) –
and the worst golf-course in the world (rough greens)!

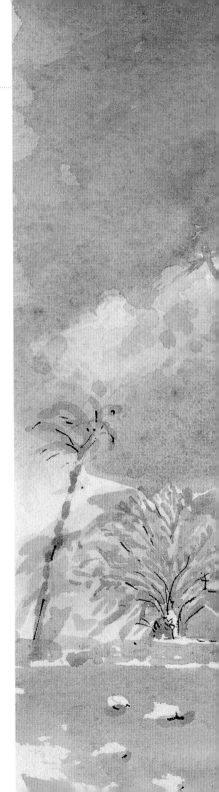

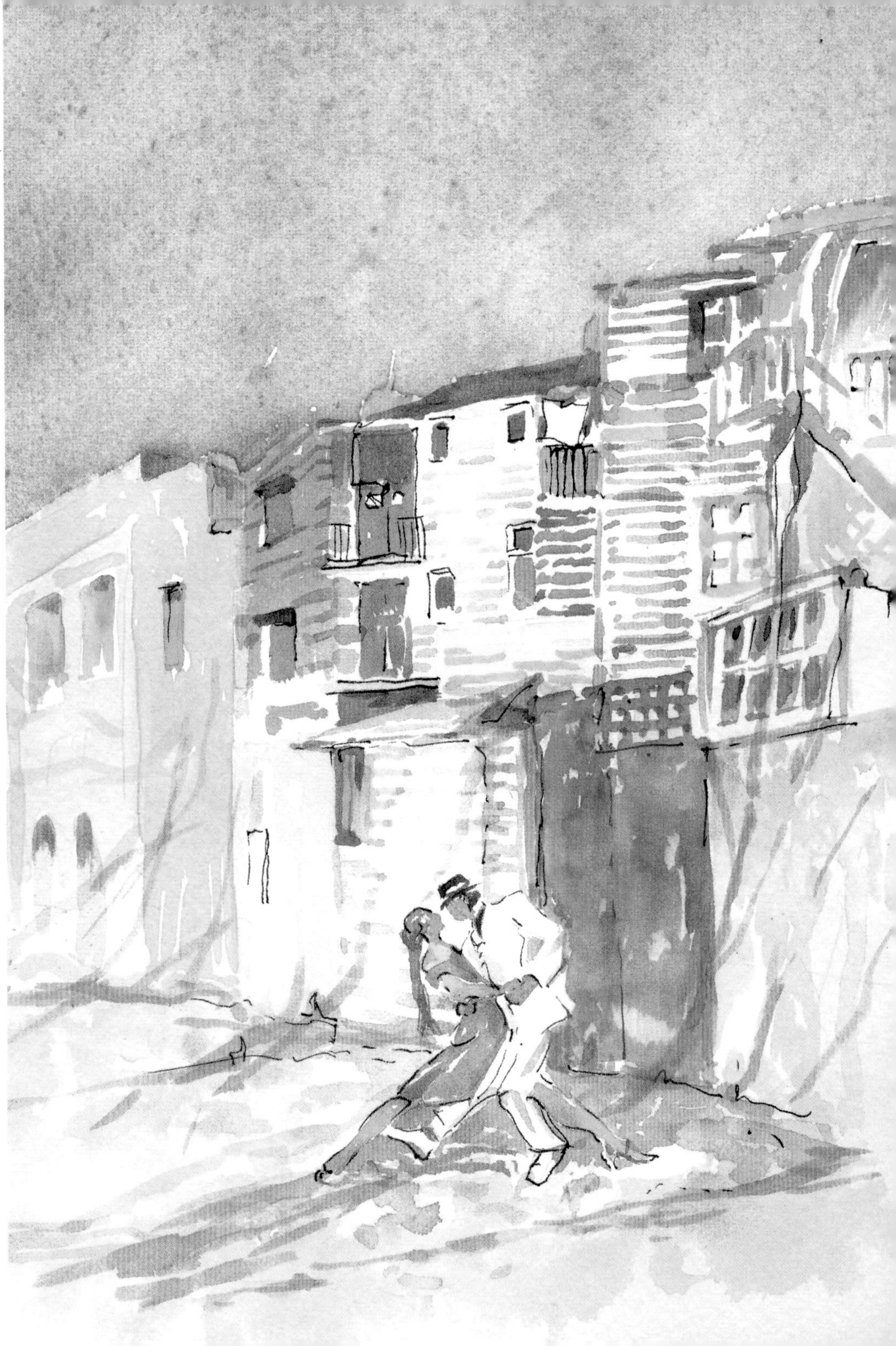

Buenos Aires

Buenos Aires – Argentina's
capital city – was called 'fair winds'
by sailors grateful to St. Mary,
Madonna di Bonaria – Sardinia is where
the name originates. The residents who crowd
this multi-cultural melting-pot
of race, religion, languages and cultures –
'the people of the port' they proudly claim to be,
and say their super city is 'the Paris
of South America'... and I remember an evening
in a dance-hall and a demonstration
of the Argentine tango (while we ate
a steak-supper) which has stayed in memory
ever since then – and always will –
unforgettable, and unforgotten.

LAGOS

The largest city in the continent
of Africa, and growing greater still –
most populous, most prosperous – a port
to match its size – Nigeria's capital:
the *Greater Lagos Metropolitan*
Region boasts more than 20 million souls.

The name means 'lakes'. The past was slaves; today,
world trade and tourists, culture and cuisine,
within this modern megacity give
Lagos the highest GDP throughout
the continent of Africa. Free trade
is what makes wealth: when will we ever learn?

In Yoruba its name is Eko; first,
a war-camp in those times of warring tribes;
today, those tribes are all the nations of the world –
and faiths, and cultures. 'Stranger-danger' makes
us fearful of each other ... which is why
free trade, and travel, also civilise.

Demerara
Shutters
Georgetown Guyana.

Georgetown

Capital of Guyana, Georgetown's on
the north-east coast of South America
beside the Demerara River-mouth,
'the Garden City of the Caribbean'.
The Dutch and French and British colonists
disputed ownership for several years:
the town, once known as Stabroek, 'standing
    pool',
assumed the name of England's George the
    Third
in 1812, and Queen Victoria
in 1842 made it a city,
protected from the ocean by a wall,
but gravely damaged by the two Great Fires
of 1945 and '51.
In 1966 the sovereign state –
Republic of Guyana – was declared,
which later chose to join the Commonwealth –
of nations in remission from the ills of empire.

The port and airport make the capital
the leading city of Guyana for
finance and commerce, government and trade.
There's lots to see: the system of canals,
the sea-wall, gardens, public buildings, parks,
the Clock Tower in the Market, and the
    Lighthouse...
and lots to learn: forget the temples, mosques
and churches – visit the Umana Yana...
and lots to ponder: cost of living, crime
(take care), the weather (warm, and wet), the
    future –
the threats of climate change and rising seas
make inundation likely before long.
Will the 'Co-operative Republic of
Guyana' find a way to save the city
by communal endeavour? We shall see
if it can raise that long sea-wall in time –
lest once more Georgetown may become a standing
pool.

[131]

THE PANAMA CANAL

The Seven Wonders of the Modern World
  comprise:
      the Golden Gate Bridge, Channel Tunnel,
      Empire State
     Building, together with a dam, a tower,
     drained Zuider Zee, and Panama Canal –
     the seven wonders of the modern world!

[132]   The greatest-ever engineering feat (so far) –
     forget the Tower of Babel, Trojan Horse,
     or Daedalus – the Panama Canal
     cost lives, and time, and funds, before it
      formed
     the greatest-ever engineering feat.

Three centuries to plan, and thirty years to build,
     begun by France, completed by the States,
     now owned and run at last by Panama –
     the tolls provide substantial revenues.
     Three centuries to plan, and thirty years...

before the first of near a million ships passed
  through
     those fifty miles – a lake, six locks (today
     there are three lanes of locks) – twelve hours
      from sea
     to sea. A floating crane took months to cross –
     before the first of near a million ships!

Enjoy the journey through this great Canal; look for
     the little engines towing giant ships;
     think of the builders, those who lived, and
      died,
     to help create this wonder of our world.
     Enjoy the journey through this great Canal.

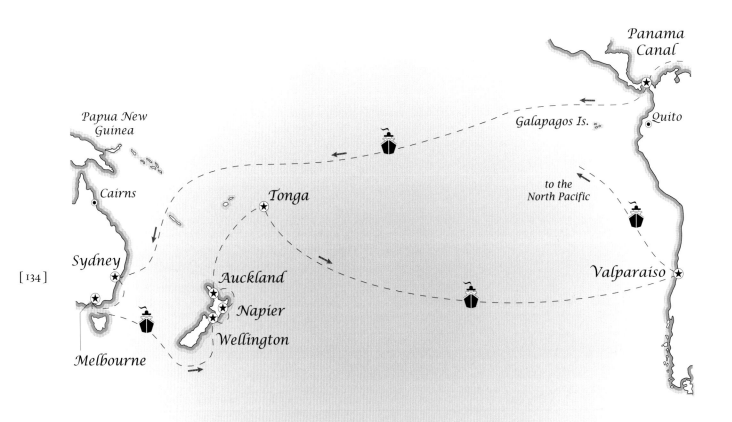

N

© S.Ballard (2021)

5. THE SOUTH PACIFIC OCEAN

The sea's a treasure-house of cowrie-shells,
star-fish and sea-glass, porpoises and prawns,
where everything's bewitched by magic spells
the water-fairies weave when day-light dawns,
and day reveals the restless ocean-swells.

The sea's a wonder-land, a water-world
of strangeness: jelly-fish and corals, whales
and walruses, brigades of breakers curled
up tight – until the water's tension fails –
to burst across the beach like sails unfurled.

The sea's a paradise land-lubbers left
behind the day our forebears crawled ashore;
since when, like Eve and Adam, quite bereft
of Eden, human-kind has yearned once more
to find our ocean-home, and feel its heft.

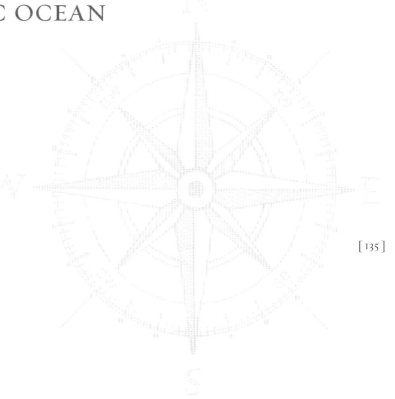

The Pacific Ocean (as a whole) is by a long way the largest of earth's oceans today. With Asia and Australia to the east, and the Americas to the west, it is almost land-locked to the north, where the narrow Bering Strait leads to the Arctic. The southern boundary is traditionally the artificial division between the Antarctic and Pacific Oceans at the 66° (and a half) south parallel. At its widest, it stretches 10,700 miles east-west, and 9,900 miles north-south. The Pacific covers twice the area of the Atlantic Ocean (64 million square miles) and contains more than double the volume of water (170 million cubic miles!). It covers an area greater (by about the size of Africa) than the entire land-surface of the earth. Watery planet, indeed!

Associated with it are a number of seas: the Bering Sea, the Sea of Japan, the Yellow Sea and the China Sea, for example. Perhaps surprisingly, relative to its size, it is fed by few great rivers: those that do drain into the Pacific include the Yukon, Columbia, Fraser and Colorado from the east, and the Yellow River and the Yangtze from the west. The area of land draining into the Pacific is merely a quarter of the area drained by the Atlantic. Like the other oceans, it is divided beneath the surface into a number of trenches or basins by irregular ridges which sometimes appear above the surface as islands: the Hawaiian Islands, for example. The average depth of the Ocean is about 13,000 feet: at its deepest point, the Challenger Depth, echo-sounders have recorded a depth of about 36,000 feet – or nearly seven miles.

The North and South Pacific are conventionally separated by the equator. They differ from one another in a number of ways, including the abundance of islands, salinity, patterns of currents and winds, character of the ocean floor, temperature and magnitude. The South Pacific Ocean is by far the largest of the world's 'seven seas'. In contrast to its northern neighbour it is crowded with islands of all sizes, from Borneo to Banks Island. The sea-floor of the North Pacific is mostly naked red clay, in contrast with the abundant sedimentary deposits in the south. The saline content of the South Pacific is roughly similar to its neighbours, the South Atlantic and Indian Oceans, whereas the North Pacific has the lowest salinity of all the seven oceans.

Our journey takes us westwards and southwards from Panama to visit some of the great Australian ports, Sydney and Melbourne; then across the Tasman Sea to call at Wellington, Napier and Auckland in New Zealand, before continuing northwards again to visit the island of Tonga, and then eastwards to Valparaiso on the coast of Chile, as our little ship makes its way towards the North Pacific.

The sea's a paradise
land-lubbers left behind
the day our forebears
crawled ashore.

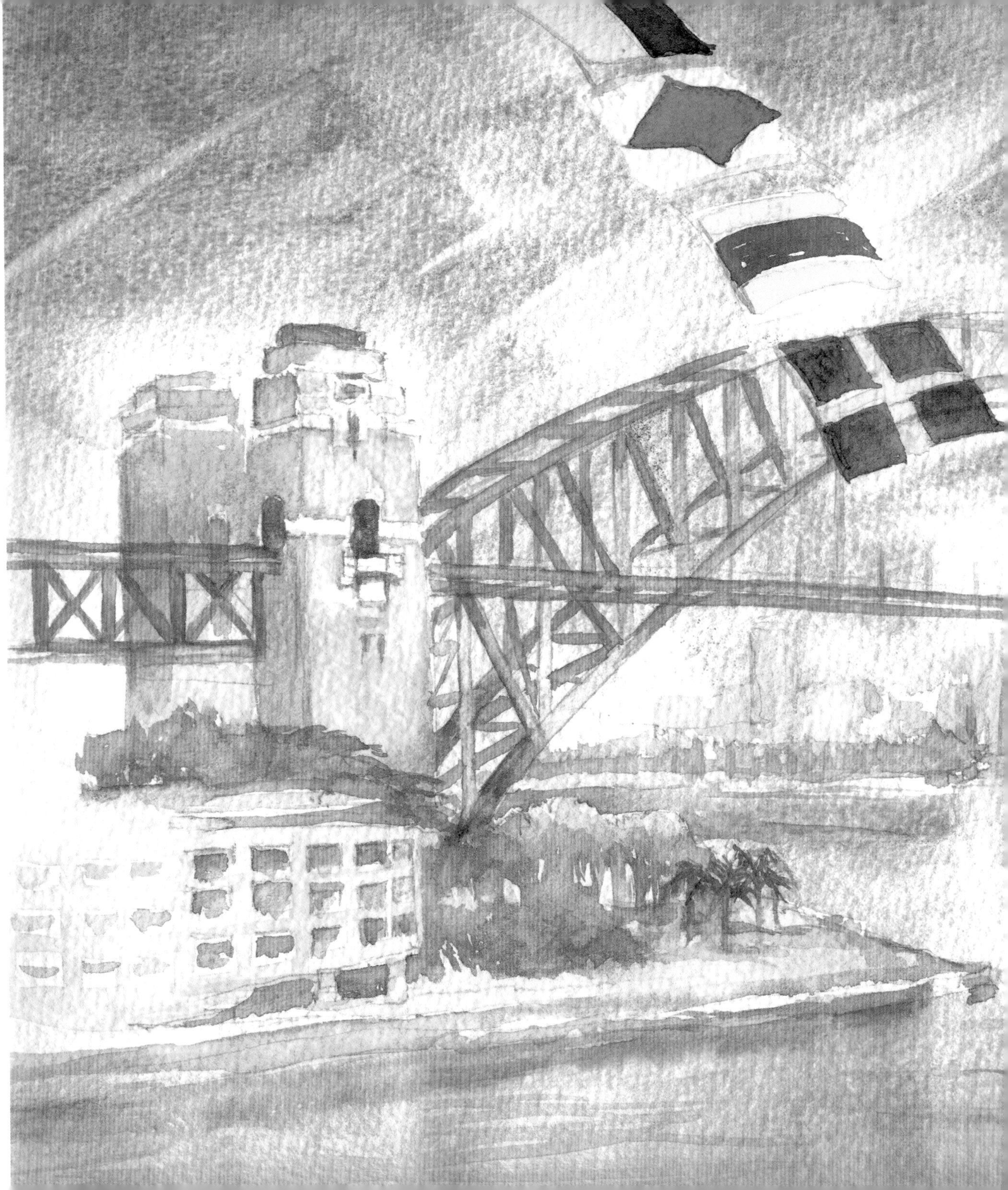

[138]

SOUTHWARDS TO SYDNEY

We wake in darkness, dress and rush on deck
to see the ship move slowly up the sound,
past sleeping suburbs, islets, homeward-bound
for Sydney's harbour after the long trek
from the chill Channel in the north.
Westwards the Bridge appears, its graceful bow
reflected in the Opera's shells below:
the city, like a maestro, now steps forth.
Beneath the stern the water foams and swirls.
We dock beside the Rocks. All motion ceased,
we stand and stare, amazed – as in the east
the glory of another dawn unfurls.

[139]

MELBOURNE

Soldiers saluted her before they went to war.
While some returned, the rest are merely names recorded
in Melbourne's Shrine. Remembrance of the one is more
affecting than memorials to the many war did
to death in our long century of warfare. Chloe,
the artist's model, died of unrequited love;
she killed herself – with poison. Nothing more to know. We
grieved for her in the tavern, where her portrait hangs above…

The individual story always moves us more
than the (mis)fortunes of the multitude. Cook's Cottage –
transported stone by stone from Yorkshire's rugged shore,
where the Cook family once supped their mess of pottage,
placed in the Fitzroy Gardens, close to Yarra Park –
of all these memorable Melbourne buildings, charmed
us with its plainness more than those the guides remark
upon – a jewel, like some fly in amber, here embalmed.

'Marvellous Melbourne' of the gold-rush days, berivalled
its sister, Sydney, for pre-eminence, and still
does – though far be it for a poet to revive old
dissensions… Melbourne is a village ('honey-rill'?)
in Derbyshire; the second Viscount of that name
was Queen Victoria's – she named the state – good friend,
Prime Minister and guide; thus, English honey came
to Oz as gold – and names a gilded City in the end.

Cook's Cottage Melbourne

Simon Lello.

Cable Car
Wellington

WELLINGTON

'Windy Wellington' – that's what they call it –
the nation's capital, but New Zealand's
second city: it's smaller than Auckland,
oddly enough – only a quarter
as many residents, but rich in heritage.
Ride the cable car, explore the country-park,
visit the museums, sample New Zealand wine.
Ponder the meaning of Maori culture,
language and customs, legends and art –
'the people of the land' for a millennium, before
the British came and conquered these islands.
But, Maori or Pakeha, man is the predator;
grieve for this 'land of glistening waters'
as you walk the paths of the Wildlife Sanctuary,
and realise that people are the problem – not the solution.

NAPIER

That high rose-window in the new
cathedral, quaint art deco shop,
neat sea-front, ice-cream parlour, view
(near where the shuttle-buses stop)

enchant the visitors, who all
admire clean streets and friendly faces,
as they explore each store and stall –
appearing to forget that places,

that earthquakes have destroyed, may be
destroyed again. This city shows
good comes from ill: but, equally,
ill follows good (the wise one knows).

Mount Eden
Aukland

AUCKLAND

'City of sparkling waters, and a hundred lovers',
of many names, and more the tourist here discovers,
who visits Akarana eager for sight-seeing,
intent on landmarks, entertainment and well-being.

Don't miss the Harbour Bridge, Museum, and Sky Tower;
Art Gallery, the parks and theatres; leave an hour
(or more) to find the City's two great universities.
(D'you think it's hard to fit all this into a verse? It is!)

Two exhibitions we enjoyed – one on volcanoes,
the other on the rights of women: man today knows
whatever needs to be known on both these explosive
topics – a good deal more than Solomon or Joseph,

who thought a woman's place was in the home – and bedroom.
Today, we must give 'equal rights for all' some headroom.
Auckland's a city that can help us learn where harm is,
to face both nature's, and society's, tsunamis.

Royal Palace
Tonga.

TONGA

The Friendly Isles: a silver band, a breeze;
the Royal Palace, Royal Tomb, and Queen
Salote's College ... gaudy cemeteries...
A land of vivid colours, blue and green,
with flame-tree blossom near a beach. We swim,
enjoy a sandwich, fruit, and dancing girl
who waves her hands — so graceful, young and slim.
She smiles — like waves, her fingers flow and curl.
John Wesley taught them Methodism: we
might learn the ordered life and friendliness
from them — their practice of equality.
Cultures change slowly; customs last. Unless
the force of conquest sets the people free,
nothing's so stubborn as ethnicity.

VALPARAISO

The various appellations of Valparaiso,
like 'Little San Francisco', or
'Jewel of the Pacific, make this city unique.
The Spanish explorers supplied the name
it bears today – 'the Dale of Paradise'.

A native village once, Valparaiso
gradually grew to become
the major city you see around you.
Prosperity came first, followed by decline,
when Panama's canal proved it redundant.

The revival of Valparaiso
arose from trade – and tourists. The earliest
of the stock exchanges established on
the continent is located here.
The dollar rules – okay! (But does it, really?)

The four universities in Valparaiso,
and twice as many technical colleges,
make this city a centre of learning.
It also preserves the oldest public
library throughout the lands of Chile.

A tourist visitor to Valparaiso
must meet 'the people of the port', explore the Metro,
take a trolley-bus, and tread the cobbles
of the ancient alleyways of the old city,
or ride the antique railway up the hills.

View the fireworks in Valparaiso
on January the 1ˢᵗ, or join the eager
audience to enjoy the 'opera by the sea'!
Here is the cultural capital of Chile,
hailed as a World Heritage Site.

Nature's violence leaves Valparaiso
in ruins (watch out!) once – or more than once –
each century. The city's owed
another earthquake any time soon...
Geology rules – and wrecks! Okay?

"Antigua Railway"
Valparaiso.

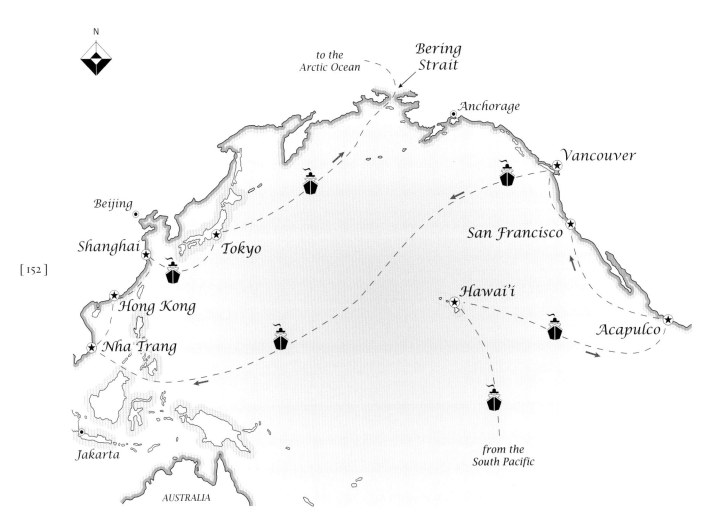

6. THE NORTH PACIFIC OCEAN

I wonder why they called it the Pacific?
'Magnificent', perhaps, 'sublime', 'terrific'
or even 'Herculean' might seem apter.
I guess I could compile a lengthy chapter

of fitter names for this unpeaceful ocean,
which night and day seems in perpetual motion
of tides and currents, surges and tsunamis,
which makes you think it doesn't know what calm is!

The Ring of Fire surrounding the tectonic
plate beneath the Pacific causes chronic
volcanic action, which disturbs the water
above the fragile crust, the sea's supporter.

The elements – air, water, earth and fire –
like joy and sadness, hatred and desire,
cannot live very comfortably together –
creating troubled feelings, and the weather.

We can't control the weather, or the oceans.
But we can learn to tame our own emotions,
our greed, and lust, and pride. To be specific,
it's people, not the sea, we need pacific.

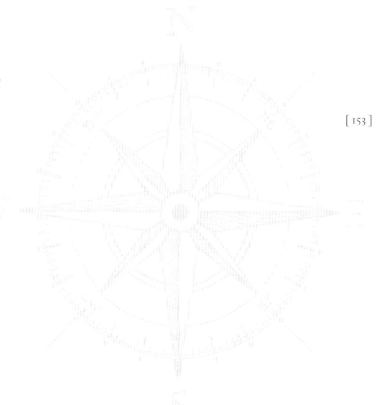

The Pacific Ocean (north and south together) is not only the world's largest and deepest ocean, almost double the area of the Atlantic – with three times as much water in it, but it is also unique due to the 'Ring of Fire' which surrounds it and makes its shores perilous. This is the result of the edges of the underlying plate constantly colliding with, sliding beneath, or rubbing against, the adjacent continental plates on which the visible world sits. These disturbances cause the earthquakes, tsunamis and volcanoes which characterise the Ocean's borders. But the Pacific also provides some of the world's most valuable resources, fish of course, coral reefs, oil and gas, and precious minerals – though the latter three are still in an early stage of exploitation and our destructive pursuit of economic progress. The noble desire to 'save the planet' is sadly fighting a losing battle with the exigencies of human greed. What the world really needs is fewer people, consuming less of the planet's resources. More easily said, than done!

In contrast to the South Pacific, where prevailing currents circulate in a counter-clockwise direction, the currents in the North Pacific move clockwise. The most important one is probably the North Equatorial Current, also known as the Japan, Black or Kuroshio Current, which is the Pacific's equivalent to the Gulf Stream in the Atlantic. In many ways the North and South Pacific mirror one another, for example in climate, currents, prevailing winds, and the presence of ice at their extremities. They share the 'Ring of Fire' and a dangerous ferocity which belies their shared name.

Our voyage continues to the north-west to Honolulu – and Pearl Harbour – in Hawai'i. Thence we sail eastwards again to the coast of Mexico and Acapulco, then northwards to San Francisco and Vancouver, before turning back towards the south and crossing the ocean to reach Nha Trang in South Vietnam, and then return northwards to visit China and Japan, before passing through the Bering Strait to enter the Arctic Ocean, the last of our Seven Seas.

We can't control the weather,
or the oceans.
But we can learn to tame
our own emotions ...

HONOLULU

Names matter. What a place or person's called
does more than just confirm identity:
while names denote, they also connotate.
Like leaves, that leave the trees in autumn? No —
like Oxford, where the cattle crossed the Thames,
or Jupiter, the god-father of Rome.
So, what on earth does Honolulu mean,
besides the place? A sheltered harbourage,
'calm port' — but not in 1941.
The 7th of December marks the day
Japan's surprise attack on nearby Pearl
Harbour persuaded the U.S. to join,
and win, the Second World War. *Victory...*
but at what cost? A tactical success,
but a strategic blunder hard to match.
Today, Hawai'i's capital, *Calm Port's*
the second safest city in the U.S.A. —
and Honolulu's name's once more appropriate!

PEARL HARBOUR

We took the tour: (Aloha, Hawai'i!)
the royal palace, statue, cemeteries,
the cliff-top viewpoint, where a battle long
ago, with spears and muskets, unified
a nation at the cost of human lives.
But how shall we remember those who died?

Pearl Harbour next – a strange memorial.
Japan's strategic blunder was a triumph
for tactics - and yet, in the end, both sides
have won. Disasters sometimes unify
nations - but always at the cost of lives.
So, how shall we remember those who died?

The Arizona lies beneath a white
memorial pontoon, bare, unadorned,
and open to the sky, and to the waves...
nothing to see, beyond a list of names;
nothing to do, apart from reading it.
Yet how shall we remember those who died?

True valour means the readiness to fight
and die, if die we must, in a good cause.
These men were brave. They sacrificed their lives,
though unaware, to make this nation one,
resolved to make the world a better place.
We shall remember them, each one who died.

La Quebra
Acapulco
Mexico.

ACAPULCO

Come fly with me – to Acapulco Bay,
Mexico's Riviera and resort;
or take a cruise to somewhere far away –
a perfect harbour, and a busy port.

Come fly with me to where the youngsters fly –
who dive from these high cliffs into the sea
to earn some dollars: most survive, some die –
while we return to sandwiches and tea.

Come fly with me to where oblivion's found
in wine, or weed – whatever turns you on –
where young Americans abound
who've come to take a trip to Babylon.

Come fly with me to where the night-life's moan
seems mournful – for a culture in decay:
those guns and gangs, the garbage thrown
into the sea ... drugs won't be wished away!

Come fly with me to Acapulco Bay,
the height of fashion, when Sinatra sang.
What yesterday was chic, today's passé:
a world ends – with a whimper, and a bang!

SAN FRANCISCO

Moored at the docks in San Francisco, we
wait patiently in line, papers in hand,
to pass through immigration and be cleared
to visit the U.S. of A. Instead,
returning to our cabin, we make tea
and take our books to sit in sunshine on
the balcony and quietly enjoy
the view: rooves in the foreground, distant hills,
and in between the bay, with Alcatraz
on one wing and the Golden Gate – more red
than gold, more like a spider's web
than any gateway – on the other side.
Traffic-noise. Sailing boats move gracefully
across the water, whilst the clear blue sky,
a little paler where it meets the hills,
provides three-quarters of what can be seen.

[164]

Vancouver
British Columbia

VANCOUVER

What makes a city? Native villages,
a natural harbour, an explorer with
a Dutch name, makeshift tavern, gold-
rush, rail-head, twenty years from starting off
to city status ... burned to ashes that
same year in June of 1886.
(But soon rebuilt, and flourishing again.)

The port, which welcomes tourists, exports logs
today. The population grew from just
a thousand to one hundred thousand in
no more than thirty years, and now has reached
six times that number in the City, and
approaches two and a half million in
Vancouver's 'local catchment area'.

A diverse population, by origin
and language, lives within this modern city –
'sustainable' and 'green' and 'liveable',
awarded many marks of quality,
attracting residents and visitors.
As cities go, it's worth a visit – since,
though young and new, Vancouver's here to stay.

NHA TRANG*

'Look out your left side hand,' our guide
instructs, 'and see Five-Star Hotel,
old Hindu Temple on the hill,
new supermarket!' But I still
prefer the sea's persistent swell
and breaking surf along the right-hand side,
the coastline threatened by the advancing tide.

So now I study both my left
and right side hands: five fingers twice,
gold wedding rings on either side,
thumb-sores and liver-spots that I'd
accepted as the usual price
of age advancing – and the life-line's cleft.
(How many years, I wonder, are there left?)

*South Vietnam

a Trang
Viet nam

Pandon L

Hong Kong

HONG KONG

I can remember Hong Kong in the old days,
when Britain's flag flew everywhere.
We stayed at Gov'ment House for seven whole days,
and studied mainland China – from the air.
aboard a helicopter with H.E.,
his watchful bodyguard, the pilot, you, and me!

After the island was returned to China,
consultant now to h.e. college clients
worldwide, I helped some visionaries design a
new Global University Alliance.
(It never pays to be among the prime
promoters of a good idea – before its time!)

Later, as tourists visiting Hong Kong, we
admired the modern Airport, scaled the Peak,
and crossed the harbour to Kowloon. (Mah Jongh we
found hard to master in one week!)
I wonder if we'll ever come again?
(But, if we do, we might be tempted to remain!)

SHANGHAI

Shanghai – the showpiece of China's economy
today – was once a Treaty Port, an outlet for
ceramics, silver, opium... and open door
for imports from the West: our manufactured goods –
and guns – and mad ideas (Marxist philosophy)...

China transforms the thoughts and things of those it meets:
in art, religion, architecture, governance
find here what's learned from others changed by choice and chance
to something unfamiliar, strange; what's understood's
reshaped; what's borrowed – once remade – often competes

with what the lender thought was good enough to gain
the gold in the great game of life... the Chinese mix
of economic freedom (much the quickest fix
for wealth creation) with severe social controls
and limited democracy works best, it's plain...

So – view the great Lokatse skyline with respect.
Forget the temples, gardens and pagodas, what
is interesting here's the present time, and not
the past – those touristic distractions. Here, your goal's
to glimpse the future – for us all... and then reflect.

Martial SingTao
Shanghai

odawara
Castle near Tokyo.

TOKYO

Today, the 'eastern capital' is Tokyo:
Kyoto was Japan's 'first city' years ago.
Before that time, a fishing village called Edo
(which means 'an estuary') began to spread and grow
into this great metropolis, where millions come and go.

The city's an Olympic venue, ranking high
among the leading cities of the world. Here's why:
for shopping, night-life, local transport – rated by
a clutch of indices – with things to satisfy
all tastes – clean, safe, hospitable. One's sad to say good-bye!

Secluded, and at peace, for centuries,
old Edo was transformed at last: a city is
changed, which endures (enjoys?) these double challenges:
a leading role, and foreign influence. But is
this half as difficult as those extreme catastrophes...

...of nature, and of war – the earthquakes and the raids
which devastated Tokyo? Touristic trade's
supreme today, along the alleys, esplanades
and avenues – the shops and stores, boutiques, arcades...
And yet we know that all things human are a dream that fades.

All nations perish in the long continuum
of history; all cities will, one day, become
ruins; and Tokyo, like Edo, must succumb
and perish in the long term (or the medium?) –
the raging fire, last time – it waits destructive floods to come.

NORTH POLE

from the
North Pacific

N

Baffin
Is.

Baffin
Bay

Svalbard

Barents Sea

Arctic Circle

Arctic Circle

Greenland

Tromso

Archangel

Reykjavik

St Petersburg

Faroe
Islands

Stockholm

Tallinn

Copenhagen

North Atlantic Ocean

Amsterdam

© S.Ballard (2021)

7. THE ARCTIC OCEAN, the North Sea and the Baltic.

A sea of ice as far as one may see
across the polar north from Europe to
America, from Asia to Qaanaaq
in Greenland – nothing more – and melting fast.
Beneath this icy sea a massive ridge,
a mountain-range submerged and never seen,
some two miles high. The Arctic is the home
of polar bears, and seals, and fish – and those
brave souls who seek to reach the northern Pole,
and live to tell the tale. (And Santa Claus.)
It's like the moon, mysterious and cold,
a cruel, harsh environment to test
the boundaries of human adaptation:
a place where tourists are as rare as rain –
a landing on the ice is not for us –
better to view it from the deck, and dream.

The Arctic Ocean takes its name from the Greek word for 'bear', a reference not to the polar bears which live there but the Great Bear, the northern constellation of stars which includes the two 'pointers', directing the eye to Polaris, the North Star. The Arctic region is usually defined as the parts of the globe to the north of the tree-line, which includes Greenland, parts of Siberia, Alaska and Canada, and the north of Iceland; but the Arctic Ocean is both larger than it seems, and more clearly defined than its southern counterpart, since the (north) polar ice-cap has no land beneath it, and the continents of North America, Europe and Asia, together with the islands of Greenland and Iceland, 'ring-fence' the Northern Ocean. Including the adjacent waters, such as the Barents Sea and the Hudson and Baffin Bays, the Arctic Ocean extends over some 5,400,000 square miles of the earth's surface, but is still ranked as the smallest of the 'seven seas'. It contains two deep basins, separated by the Lomonosov ridge-system.

Until recently, the polar ice-cap, which forms the massive centre of the Ocean, extended to meet the lands of the surrounding islands and continents, making it difficult in summer (and impossible in winter) to navigate either 'the north-west passage' (above Canada and Alaska) or 'the north-east passage' (above Europe and Siberia); but global warming has now melted the edges of the ice-cap to such an extent that the encircling seas of The Arctic Ocean are fully open to shipping – though, remembering the fate of *The Titanic*, it is still advisable to keep a good look-out for icebergs. The temperature of the water rarely rises above 5° C. Swimming is not an Arctic sport for humans.

The Arctic is rich in natural resources, such as coal, oil, gas, and fish, which have been ruthlessly exploited in the past; today, quota systems have been introduced to encourage more responsible mining and fishing. Inevitably, the native inhabitants – the Nenets of Russia, European Lapps, and North American Inuit, together with indigenous herds of reindeer – have suffered from the damage to their traditional lifestyles and the pollution of the environment. Progress always comes at a price.

The North Sea and the Baltic are properly tributary seas of the North Atlantic Ocean, but it is convenient to mention them here. They lie to the south of the Norwegian Sea, itself part of the Northern Ocean. The North Sea links the Arctic to the Atlantic Ocean, and is of relatively recent origin. During the Tertiary Period the low-lying land connecting Britain to the continent gradually sank below the level of the oceans to create a shallow sea, rich in fish. Before that happened the Thames was apparently a mere tributary of the Rhine. The Straits of Dover appeared as late as the last Ice Age in about 10,000 BCE – to complete a kind of 'geological Brexit'. Fed by the Baltic and a multitude of rivers, the North Sea is rather less salty then the Atlantic. Though cold, as intrepid east-coast swimmers know, it never freezes.

The Baltic Sea (*Ostsee*, 'eastern sea', in German) extends over slightly more than 165,000 square miles, and was once a vast fresh-water inland lake – before the channel between Sweden and Denmark (the Skagerrak and Kattegat) opened as recently as 6,500 BCE. Like the North Sea, it is relatively shallow; large ocean liners must navigate it with care, or not at all. It is one of the least saline regions of the world's ocean-system – in places the water is almost drinkable.

As a result, the ports around the Baltic are often frozen up during the winter, and marine life is relatively impoverished – perhaps no more than one-tenth as varied and extensive as in the North Sea. The inflow of fresh water from the rivers draining into the Baltic raises the sea-level in places by up to 40 centimetres above that of the North Sea and the Atlantic; even in the Kattegat, which connects the Baltic to the North Sea, the difference is some 10 centimetres – which means there is a continual outflow from east to west. While the North Sea is tidal, the Baltic has no noticeable tidal variation.

Our journey around the ice-cap starts from the Bering Sea at the northern tip of the Pacific and proceeds clockwise, skirting the northern boundaries of Asia, Europe and America in turn, and visiting Archangel, a north Russian port, and Greenland before turning back to call at Reykjavik in Iceland, then sailing southwards through the North Sea to enter the Baltic, and finally returning to Amsterdam and Greenwich – and home in the UK.

[177]

Archangel

ARCHANGEL

Named for St. Michael who, they like to say,
defeated the Great Devil near this spot –
the coat of arms records the deed today –
but who can tell if legends lie, or not?

Archangel's history starts with Vikings who
left treasure here a thousand years ago.
Norway and Russia struggled to subdue
the region, till the Tsar dispatched the foe,

and unified the Russian state. The port,
originally a busy trading post,
became in World War II a haven sought
by Allied convoys off the Arctic coast.

Today, a major sea-port (timber, fish)
available year-long, thanks to the ice-
breakers' new power (and the ice-melt – I wish
it were not so). What does not change is vice.

The world, the flesh, the devil, we are told,
are constant lures to lead the weak astray.
The world's the common herd, whose vice-like hold
exerts its grip by normalising grey

to seem like white (and black, as grey); the flesh –
our appetites, desires and lust,
which, never satisfied, revive afresh
each day, each night, in spite of shame, disgust

or sermons. But the devil is the worst –
our own habitual behaviours, which
can make our lives feel wretched and accursed –
Auden's 'intolerable neural itch'.

St. Michael, the archangel, who fought well,
and crushed the devil, must be quite the most
famous inhabitant of Archangel,
and one of whom they've every right to boast!

[179]

GREENLAND

Like Iceland – mostly cloaked in ice – Greenland
is hardly green! The name was chosen by
Erik the Red, who hoped it might attract
more migrants, all in vain. Those early Norse
inhabitants found life in Greenland harsh
and brief – the old and the infirm were killed,
their bodies flung from cliffs into the sea –
and in the 15th century the last
brave settlers withdrew. The Eskimos
remained – they knew how to survive the cold.

The Portuguese came next – and quickly left!
Then Denmark's king dispatched a fleet to claim
possession: Danish sovereignty survives
today (in principle), though Home Rule has
become *de facto* ... independence is
one step away. In 1985
Greenland arranged to 'Gr-exit' the E.U.,
although the Danes remain in membership.
(Perhaps they might advise the U.K. how
to have its cake and eat it one day soon!)

The largest island in the world (don't count
Australia – a continent), Greenland's
interior is mostly ice, the land
beneath's largely submerged below the sea,
as global warming and the melting ice
will soon reveal. In time, all climates change –
for Greenland has been warm and fertile in
the past – and will be so again. Perhaps, before
the century is done, we'll wish to stay –
and Greenland may become a green land yet!

REYKJAVIK

This *steamy city*'s name connotes 'hot springs'
(and night-life) – where the Norsemen settled first
a thousand years ago, and more. The King
of Denmark gave it city-status in
1786, and it became
the capital of Iceland when the old
assembly, *Alþingi,* the parliament
created centuries before, was moved
from Thingvellir in 1845.
Icelandic independence came at last
in 1918, but the years between
the two World Wars were hard for Reykjavik
until, once Germany had occupied
Denmark, four British warships (peacefully)
invaded Iceland, though a neutral state,
and brought prosperity, development –
and soldiers from the U.S.A. What was
a village once became a modern city,
with economic growth. Those 'Tiger Years'
concluded with the crash of 2008.
And now, the third (peaceful) invasion – by
the tourists, flocking to explore one of
the cleanest, greenest, safest cities in
the world today – provides prosperity
once more for chilly, cloudy Reykjavik.
Invasion isn't always a disaster...

STOCKHOLM

Stockholm's name denotes an 'island fort',
which grew to be the largest city in
the Nordic region in a thousand years:
today, a thousand thousand residents work here.

Sweden's capital is both a port
and busy city, clean and green, within
which we may find both food for thought (ideas)
and food to taste, and sights to see, and much to cheer.

Strindberg's city, where the royal court
and government reside; the park, wherein
the bones of Greta Garbo lie, endears
it most to me – of all the varied riches here.

Scandinavia's more than winter sport,
the Vikings, sagas, lays of Hnæf and Finn,
those open sandwiches and souvenirs.
What Stockholm offers – we should study, and revere.

Gamalin
Square
Stockholm.

Little Mermaid
Copenhagen

COPENHAGEN

A fishing village once, the capital
of Denmark now, but in between both plague
and fire – and Nelson's fierce assault – and all
the pain of Nazi occupation in
the years of World War II… this city's seen
more suffering than most: but, phoenix-like,
or like The Little Mermaid on the rock,
it has revived – re-planned, rebuilt and strong.
The Bridge (to Sweden) and the Opera House
are two of many 'must-see' sights. With parks
and gardens everywhere, the city's 'green'
(in every sense) and user-friendly, safe,
outstanding for its quality of life:
sample the open sandwiches and beer,
those Danish pastries – and the local fish.

[187]

TALLINN

A city with a multitude of names:
Qaleven, Kolyvan and Ledenets
(maybe...), but Reval first, then Tallinn claims
authority. Place-names are epithets,
characterising places: Tallinn means
'the Danish fort' – suggesting might-have-beens.

Estonia one hundred years ago
at last gained independence ... not for long.
Both Germany and Russia had a go
at annexation, but an ancient wrong
was righted in the 'singing revolution',
establishing a sovereign constitution

in 1991. Since when, Tallinn
has flourished as a global city – Skype
and other major companies have been
created here (you *should* believe the hype!) –
not long ago one of Europe's 'Capitals
of Culture' – crowded with memorials,

museums, churches – it is now a World
Heritage Site. This 'Singing Nation' holds
a festival of song, when all are whirled
back to that special year (the story told's
the truth!) when music mastered might,
and singing won the day, without a fight.

Tallinn

ST. PETERSBURG

Another city with a dozen names –
this *Window to the West*, and *City of
Three Revolutions*, was first called (by Peter
the Great) *St Peterburg*, but the Great War
transformed the name to *Petrograd*; the death
of Lenin changed this name to *Leningrad* –
which lasted until 1991,
when the original *St Peterburg*
(*St Petersburg* in English – with an s)
resumed the role, though local residents
refer to *Piter* – sort of Russian *Brum*!
I wonder if the name will ever change again?

The second greatest Russian city, with
more than five million people living there,
St. Petersburg's the cultural capital
of Russia: Pushkin, Gogol, Nabokov
and Dostoyevsky (just to name a few);
The Hermitage (besides two hundred more
museums!); film – *Anna Karenina*
and countless others; dance – Nijinsky and
Pavlova, Nureyev, Ulanova
and many more who graced the Kirov stage.
Now a UNESCO site of heritage,
I think this *second city*'s culture leads the world!

Cruise on the Neva river, walk the streets –
the Nevsky Prospekt – find the Winter Palace,
the tallest building (and the largest mosque)
in Europe, churches and canals: recall
St. Petersburg is also sometimes called
The Venice of the North, with water-ways
and bridges everywhere – a city crammed
with treasures, most in public view, but some
concealed from all except the curious few,
like Caedmon's Hymn, the first recorded verse
in English: here's the earliest extant
copy, still urging us to praise the works of God.

A Dutch Tragedy

Near Amsterdam, in Volendam
one hundred years ago,
the Hotel Spaander offered studios
to struggling artists, who would sometimes pay
their bills with paintings. Now, the restaurant
is filled with pictures (good and bad) which show
the life of Holland – windmills, seascapes, boats,
those Dutch interiors, the furnishings and dress –
one hundred years ago
in Volendam near Amsterdam.

Near Amsterdam, in Volendam
one hundred years have passed
since Georg Hering settled his account
with two indifferent portraits: one, a child
in Dutch traditional costume with a doll;
the other, the betrothal of a girl
in a green bonnet with a man who smokes,
seeming complacent still today, although
one hundred years have passed
in Volendam near Amsterdam.

Near Amsterdam, in Volendam
one hundred long years past,
young Georg married Pauline Spaander, who
was then the daughter of the house. They are
the couple in the picture; the sweet child –
their daughter, Dorothea. Pauline died.
The painter promptly wed another woman,
who drowned his little daughter in the well,
one hundred long years past
in Volendam near Amsterdam.

Volendam Holland.

Royal Observatory
Greenwich

Simon Lello

GREENWICH*

Like flies in amber, we are locked in time.
Our island is encompassed by the sea.
Greenwich provides the home and history
of seafaring, the origin and prime
marker of latitude and measurement
of time; teaches what Mean Time means – and meant

to sailors. Here's the oldest Royal Park,
Royal Observatory, the Museum,
the Queen's House: each explains why tourists come
to Greenwich. Don't forget the *Cutty Sark*,
the last of the great ships that brought us tea
from China. And there's even more to see.

Visit the Market, and the famous inn,
Trafalgar Tavern, by the river, and
the Royal Naval College, which was planned
by Wren, replacing an old palace, in
which were born two Tudor Queens and King
Henry, their father, during England's spring.

England today's autumnal. It's the fall
of a long year of enterprise and glory.
People come here to read that splendid story
of past achievements. Query: is that all
we have to offer now? Not quite. Stand on
the starting line of London's Marathon.

This poem was first published in 'That Mighty Heart, Visions of London', 2014.

ENVOI - A SESTINA OF WATER*

Η θάλασσα, Η θάλασσα. ('The sea! The sea!').
Xenophon, *The Anabasis*

We drop through waterfalls down to an ocean
of sunlight and air. Suddenly grateful
for faces and voices, we feed upon raindrops
of milk and attention, immersed in rivers
of sleep and love, starting life's journeys
fellowed by water – a friend that proves lasting.

Playing with water yields pleasures lasting
a lifetime: watching waves in the ocean
from perilous shores, or ships on their journeys;
swimming or sailing; the sea makes us grateful.
Water's our playmate in pools and rivers,
or gardens nourished by glistening raindrops.

Water works for us too: wells fed by raindrops,
kettles and cisterns – the simple everlasting
water-cycle: seas, clouds, rivers
turning mill-wheels as they marathon to the ocean;
hydro-electric heating at home; we are grateful
for canals and sea-lanes providing safe journeys.

The four elements are never absent from our journeys
through life – fire, earth, air and raindrops.
One and all seem miraculous. Each makes us grateful.
But water is wizardry outlasting
familiarity, a single drip or the deepest ocean.
We're distracted by streams, astonished by rivers.

Water's a friend – but also a foe: rivers
may flood, and ships founder on journeys
amidst menacing mountains of ocean.
Such damage and destruction from delicate raindrops!
Water wrecks, and renews – for nothing is lasting:
a natural wonder of the world. Be grateful…

for the bewildering metamorphoses of water – grateful
for snowfalls and icebergs, salmon-filled rivers,
storm-clouds and mist on the mountains lasting
day-long, steam power for Stephenson's journeys,
hot sulphur springs, sparkling raindrops,
still tarns feeding the eternal ocean.

Learn to be grateful on life's journeys
for the mysteries of rivers and the magic of raindrops,
as you seek lasting solace in the ocean.

[197]

*This poem was first published, entitled 'Outward Bound', in 'That Strange Necessity, Visions of Portmeirion', 2015.

ACKNOWLEDGEMENTS

First of all, we wish to acknowledge, and record our gratitude for, the support and assistance provided by our partners, Wendy – who has carefully proof-read and commented on the work in progress – and John, who sadly died before it was complete, but would surely have been our first, and fairest, critic.

Secondly, we gratefully thank our publisher, James Ferguson, the designer of the book, Andrew Esson, and Sebastian Ballard who skilfully created the maps of the seven oceans, without whom this book would not have been possible

Lastly, we record our thanks to Wendy Ball for her generous Foreword, and those who have advised us on various parts of this book, including Dr. Andrew Ball, who has advised his brother on scientific and technical matters in the Introduction. Of course, we take full responsibility for any errors and infelicities that remain.

Learn to be grateful on life's journeys
for the mysteries of rivers
and the magic of raindrops,
as you seek lasting solace
in the ocean.

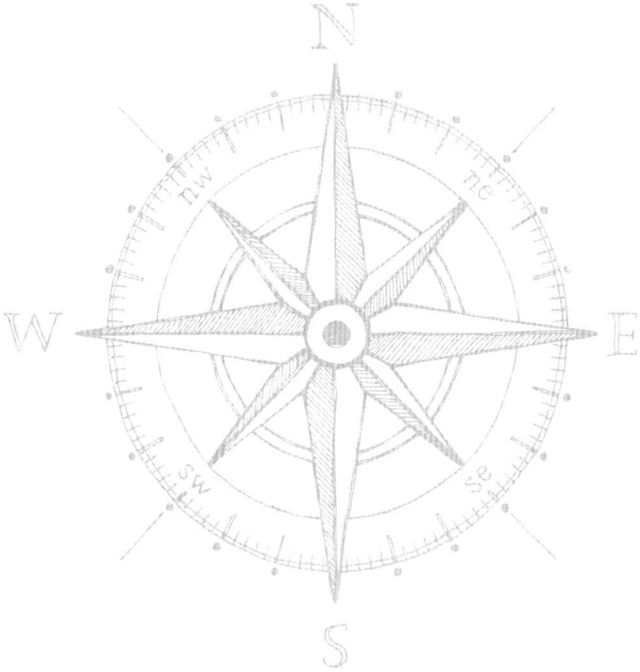
N
nw
ne
W
E
sw
se
S